DON'T TELL MUM

DON'T TELL MUM

Hair-raising messages home from gap-year travellers

Simon Hoggart and Emily Monk

Atlantic Books
London

Published in hardback in Great Britain in 2006 by Atlantic Books.
Atlantic Books is an imprint of Grove Atlantic Ltd.

Illustrated by Scott Garrett/Heart

Printed in Great Britain

ISBN 10: 1 84354 539 X
ISBN 14: 978 1 84354 539 2

Atlantic Books
An imprint of Grove Atlantic Ltd
Ormond House
26-27 Boswell Street
London
WC1N 3JZ

Contents

Introduction

It is one of the milestone events in a modern parent's life. You get to the airport with your child. It is possibly the first time they have left home for more than a few days. Even if they have been away to school, they have always been near helpful, protective adults who make sure they are fed, watered, clean and safe. What's more, it seems only a few months ago that they were toddlers, taking their first steps, saying their first words.

Now they are going alone into a wider, more frightening world. They are probably less anxious than you, which is important, because you are very anxious indeed. Every article you read describing backpackers being murdered by drug smugglers in Thailand, or falling off South American mountains, is about your child. Never mind that dozens of your friends have got their offspring back safely after many adventures – some of which were, admittedly, terrifying, bizarre, or merely the result of their own stupidity. Never mind that at the school's gap-year briefing session, the teacher smiled comfortingly and said, 'Well, we haven't lost anyone yet!' They are going thousands of miles away, into the unknown, and you won't be there to help.

Then the long-feared moment of parting. I can still see my own eighteen-year-old daughter's brave smile as she had her boarding pass checked on the way into the departure lounge, a place where there are many retail opportunities but no hugs. You realize that, in a way, your entire life is going to be on hold until the moment a few months later the same child emerges from

Customs. And that is another landmark moment, especially when, back at home, they unpack a cascade of presents – souvenirs, packets of strange spices, letter openers, a cufflink box made from the skin of a crocodile, brass candlesticks, a liqueur made from fermented cactuses, leather elephants decorated with coloured beads, recipe books which would be wonderful if you could find any of the ingredients at Sainsbury's. There are great drifts of photographs: 'this was our guide through the caves'; 'these are all the kids in my class'; 'he was that boy I told you about'; 'this was the view from the top, I'm afraid it was a bit misty that day ...' Of course you don't care that it was misty – you're just overwhelmed with relief that they are safely back under your roof again.

Then there is at least forty-eight hours before the first row ('you've only been back two days and already your room is a tip') and, over the weeks and months, the realization that your child has subtly changed, become a little more assured and self-reliant, a mite less cynical, slightly more aware of the world around them – in other words, more mature. That, too, is an important moment.

Gap years are not new, though the term itself is recent. It is defined as a period of time between leaving school and going on to higher education, though it's not uncommon now for people to have a gap year – sometimes their second – after graduating and before starting work. Some people even interrupt their careers in midflow for a gap, and a handful of them appear in this book. I would guess, and there are no supporting figures, that around half of gappers go to a particular place to do a specific job, working voluntarily for board and lodging, though some are paid pocket money. Several companies now offer a placement service, matching the student to the job, and providing a level of supervision, rather like tour reps. These schemes tend to be expensive, and not always worth the money. Other students only want to travel, usually as back-packers, sometimes alone, more often with good friends – who may or may not remain good friends through their travels.

I did mine a long time ago. The university I went to made it a condition that I spent a year doing something else before starting (they didn't say 'get yer knees brown' but that's roughly what they meant), so in 1965 I went to teach in western Uganda, at a school in the foothills of the Ruwenzoris, the Mountains of the Moon. The school was a Scottish Presbyterian foundation, and the pupils (quite a few of whom were older than me) wore khaki kilts and goatskin sporrans. I learned a lot of things in my six months, not all pious truths about the relationship between the rich and the Third World, or the burning desire of impoverished young people to be educated. For instance, I discovered that I was a lousy teacher, something that has helped me throughout my life since I have never again taken teaching work. I found out a great deal about people's priorities, not least from a staff meeting at which we spent five minutes deciding to spend a vast sum on a new chapel, then the next fifty-five minutes on whether boys who broke their garter elastic should be given sixpence for more, on the grounds that it was weak garter elastic, or made to buy their own since they had probably snapped it making catapults. The issue split the school.

But the main difference with today is communication. Every week I wrote home on one of those flimsy blue aerograms. ('Went with the athletics team to Kampala. Chaka, the captain, was found with several packets of cigarettes in his kit bag ...

camped in the Queen Elizabeth game park and chased a hippo – which was really stupid.') Most weeks a letter arrived from my parents, written at regular intervals but often arriving in bunches. News of the greater world could be obtained from the bound week's copies of the *Daily Mirror*, sold at Bimji's general store long after the events they described. And, of course, from the invaluable BBC World Service. I can still recall the excitement of hearing the Stones's 'Satisfaction' for the first time on the games master's scratchy radio, tuned to the UK Top Twenty show.

Now there are internet cafés in the smallest, poorest and most miserable towns in the world, and for some travellers a visit has become part of their daily routine. Usually they are not expensive, though gappers tend to be obsessed by money, walking miles to save a few pence on a bus fare, regarding a visit to KFC as a rare indulgence (though there usually seems to be enough money for drink and, slightly less often, drugs). For anxious parents the internet is a tremendous boon. The relief of opening an email that starts, 'Hi Mum, Hi Dad, having a great time ...' is like a sugar rush. On the other hand, you can easily take the stream of messages for granted, and come near to panic when it's interrupted. Close friends of ours had a son who went travelling in north-western India with a companion. The parents knew they'd been heading for a city which had just been struck by a terrible earthquake. For several grim days they heard nothing, the bubble of fear rising and falling inside them. But when the next cheery email arrived it explained that the earthquake had destroyed communications in the area and a tummy bug had prevented them from going to the city in the first place.

On the other hand, an email that does arrive can produce just as much terror. The idea for this book came from a friend of mine whose son was travelling around Thailand. 'Dear Mum and Dad,' he wrote, 'have just been swimming with the sharks – not as dangerous as it sounds! Off to Angkor Wat tomorrow, but none of the guys wants to come, so I'll be on my own. See you at Heathrow on Thursday!' My friend described anaesthetizing her brain with wine before going to sleep, then regaining consciousness at one in the morning, knowing she would be awake for the rest of the night. Of course, her boy arrived back at Heathrow right on time, vaguely puzzled that anyone should have been concerned.

I thought then that the sheer energy and verve in gap-year emails would make a fascinating, funny and occasionally terrifying book, though I couldn't figure out how to assemble the material. Emails are, after phone calls, the most ephemeral of all communications, and only a handful of parents bother to keep them. Then, in December 2005, I was at one of those charity Christmas 'fayres', going through the bookstand, and found a pamphlet called *Dear Mum*, written by Emily Monk. It was just thirty-two pages, and sold at £3, with profits going to a school for the very poorest children in Ghana. Like all newspaper columnists, I am usually desperate for material, and the emails in the booklet were all I had hoped – witty, crazy, improbable, wildly exaggerated no doubt, full of life and the hectic, tumbling excitement of discovering the world. Several hundred people wrote in to buy the booklet, selling out the print run. Then it turned out that we and Emily's parents had mutual friends, so it was easy to get together and plan this much longer book. Of the many hundreds of emails from which it is compiled, probably half come from Emily's friends, and friends of friends of friends, since the magic of electronic mail means that someone sitting in a café in Peru can send a message to New Zealand, which is then passed on to West Africa, and then finally winds up two days later in another café in Vietnam – where, as it happens, Emily spent a chunk of her own gap year in 2006.

Reading the material has been a constant delight. The verve, the guts, the sheer roistering enjoyment of these kids! Some, of course, had a horrible time at first, unable to adjust, desperately missing home. But in almost all cases it's possible to track how they came first to tolerate, then to relish, the places they find themselves in and the people and cultures they encounter. Anyone who fears for our future can take encouragement from these emails. This is a generation which appears to know no fear, full of young men and women who dance on the edge of volcanoes, go bungee jumping into canyons, hitch-hike through China, live among cattle with the Masai in Kenya, face down Mongolian immigration officials, saunter insouciantly into jungles, paddle canoes down piranha-infested rivers, cope with Russian mafia types, and generally display magnificent courage, resource and, sometimes, idiocy.

I have no doubt that some of the stories told here are exaggerated for effect (though none of them strike me as having been made up from nothing). I'm just as sure that some of the events have been toned down, if only for the benefit of fretful parents. We do promise that every single extract here is from a genuine email. We have, of course, had to cut them down, leaving in the highlights, and we have tinkered with both spelling and punctuation, since many of the emails were typed at breakneck speed, and would be incomprehensible without these very adjustments. For most of these kids punctilious spelling and the use of semi-colons would be as great a luxury as a hot bath, or a full English breakfast. That's not why they are where they are. We have also changed all the names.

For the benefit of those who don't have children aged between seventeen and twenty-two, here is a glossary of some common words which you will find in the following pages and which might cause momentary puzzlement. Few are politically correct:

action usually refers to sex. 'No action yet, but I have hopes of this blond boy with a tongue piercing.'

annoying a very pejorative term. In adult-speak, it might refer to a wasp or a traffic jam. To gappers it means a deeply painful person. Not to be confused with **arsey** which means deliberately offensive and aggressive, as in 'this arsey policeman moved us on.'

fit (adj.), fittie (noun) little to do with physical health; instead, 'sexually attractive person'.

gay has lost its specific meaning, and is now just an all-purpose term of abuse. 'A gay bar' is merely a bad bar, not one frequented by homosexuals.

gos (sometimes **goss** or **goz**): gossip.

hardcore serious, committed, over-the-top. 'He drank 10 pints in an hour, just to show he was hardcore.'

lame (sometimes noun, **lamo**) feeble, not up to scratch. 'Being a complete lamo I didn't join in the bungee jump.'

minging once used against any ill-favoured woman. Now a general term of abuse.

minted wealthy. 'Tom's friends are minted, and live in this wicked house overlooking the beach.'

phat a term of approval. 'The dive at the reef was phat.'

quaint strange, unexpected, unusual. Nothing to do with 'old-fashioned'. 'We went to this quaint dinner at Ho's brother's house…'

random inexplicable, haphazard. 'The bus driver read our palms for us. How random is that?'

randommers strangers encountered along the way. 'These randommers we met on the train offered to put us up for the night.'

rank disgusting.

rents (sometimes **'rents**): parents.

retard usually refers to anyone who annoys the gapper or gets in his way. 'This bunch of retards took our passports then refused to give them back.'

safe another term of approval.

skank utterly disgusting, and probably stinking as well.

wicked all-purpose term of approval. 'The beach party was wicked.'

So, here they are, the flower of our youth. All of them know that in a few weeks or months they are going to be dividing their lives between the university library and the students' union bar. Three or four years later they will probably be firmly lodged in the world of work. In the meantime they plan to stock up on fun, on experience and on life – more than they will ever be able to remember. And if they discover themselves too, well, that's an unexpected bonus.

If you receive similar emails, which you feel deserve a wider audience, do send them to us, via the publishers. There may well be a second volume.

The Call of the Weird

The whole and entire point of a gap year is to have bizarre experiences of the type you could never have at home, will almost certainly never have again, and in the majority of cases, would never want to have again. This is from a girl in India.

✉ I have been in a Bollywood film!!! They're desperate for extras at the moment, no Westerners anywhere, so the minute you step out of the door in the morning you're bombarded with agents, it's like being famous! So we agreed with this blokey to do a film that would involve being put up in a 5-star hotel for 2 nights in a place outside Mumbai … sounds too good to be true, actually lots of people we've met have done similar things, so we thought we would give it a shot. Except it was too good to be true. He picked us up in the evening and drove us to this random area in the suburbs to get a luxury bus. Along the way we learned that it wasn't a film, but a real marriage where we had to meet and greet the guests, not as attractive to us as a film, especially when he said we had to particularly greet the young men. Then the luxury Volvo coach with air-con, TV and reclining seats turned out to be a dodgy minivan parked down a back alley. Decided there was no chance we'd be getting on that bus, jumped into the nearest taxi with the guy running after us telling the taxi driver not to drive off.

But they were undeterred in their quest for stardom. Soon afterwards they found work as extras with twenty other Westerners.

✉ They produced these clubbing clothes for us to wear, sequins, leather hotpants, see-thru dresses, we all laughed in disbelief until we realized they were serious. Sadly I forgot my camera so won't be able to show you how I looked in my red sequined dress! Anyway, basically we spent half a day rolling with sweat, doing a stupid dance move to these even stupider dancers. Oh yeah, and I got told off by the chief choreographer, quite proud of that, a little claim to fame. All that for 500 rupees, that's about £6, quite a good wage in India …

A poignant email from a young woman in Pakistan.

✉ Darling Mummy and Daddy, it's Saturday and I'm sitting outside the post office. Every hour or so a marriage procession will pass underneath, whereby the woman is carried, in all her splendour, on a portable chair beneath an umbrella. The band hoots and clangs and is leading the procession of villagers. At first it seemed wonderful, but if you look at the young bride's face underneath her veil she is invariably crying and exuding the dreadful expression of one who is aware she is about to enter an agonizing contract. It's harrowing. Since leaving England, I have grown to admire and respect the amazing different cultures we have briefly sampled. Arranged marriages, however, seem incomprehensible. Despite this, last night I met a very happy couple who have been married for 29 years, following an arranged marriage. I guess it's lucky I'm not a Muslim.

This from a young man in India.

✉ Two weeks ago we went to a circumcision party in the village, a serious blast and a half. The poor guy had a marquee put up to celebrate the loss of his most tender parts. We were treated like royalty, and majorly spiced out on the whole chilli I was made to eat. They all watch you eating … weird. Last week I went to the village cricket match and was made to be the commentator on the loudspeaker for ten minutes. I was put in the royal box and everything. Still no chicks around, wondering whether to strut my stuff in the village. Hmmm, apparently we'll get lynched if we try any moves. But I'm having more fun than all of you. Toodle-pip, Gav

This adventurous young man visited Iran and found himself living the news.

✉ Tehran passed by in a flash. I took an exceptionally uncomfortable overnight train to Esfahan. I was woken by the dawn prayer stop so walked up and down the carriages. A friendly man pointed out Iran's nuclear facility that is causing such chagrin in the West. It was surrounded by a line of sandbagged anti-aircraft guns manned by two un-uniformed men, two per gun. The man who showed me this asked me what I thought of it, and we had a long and convivial, if guarded on my part, discussion. It seems to have become an issue of face. Whether by accident or design he and his friends have a perception that Iran is the only country in the world without nuclear capabilities.

Esfahan is a tourist city without any tourists. It has a long and glorious history, with ornate mosques, gardens, palaces and museums. It has restaurants that look like they come out of Disneyland, and seemingly more gift and souvenir shops than anywhere I have been. I went to a beautiful medieval mosque one afternoon. It had had six visitors that day … one day I went to use the computers in the slick new library and decided to make use of the lavatories in the basement. My Farsi isn't up to much, so I went to a bathroom and, seeing it was empty, presumed it would be all right to make use of it. Imagine my horror as I squatted away in a cubicle and heard the chatter of some women. In Iran, one of the most sensitive countries on this issue, I was making use of the ladies' loo. Chances are, if you get caught doing something like that, you get your hands chopped off. And Iranian ladies are just like ladies in Europe or America. Once they get chatting there's no stopping them. So I was trapped for half an hour, praying that nobody would knock on the door of my cubicle.

Politics rarely intrudes into the lives of our gappers, but when it does it can be embarrassing. Imagine that your child was in Nepal and they reported back that everything was just fine – except they had been seized by a group of revolutionary guerrillas.

⊠ We first encountered the Maoists about a month into the placement. Somewhere along the line what actually happened got a bit distorted. To say we were held hostage would be overshooting the mark, although technically it's true. We all went to get the 11 a.m. bus into Ghorabi, and as we approached the place where the bus sits and waits we were surrounded by six men, none older than us, brandishing 1960s' Kalashnikov rifles. They told us to sit down (we did) and that we were not allowed to leave until the rally, which we had inadvertently stumbled upon, was finished.

It was scary, they were painfully young and they had

guns which they chose to point at us. So for four hours we sat and listened and watched while these Maoists preached their message to the masses. After the initial fear wore off, it simply became a bit boring. We couldn't understand what was being said, and it lasted a long time. When it was finished we walked home, and that was that.

For some people, Australia is already as familiar as their homes. This young man went to Melbourne.

✉ Hi guys, I have been here for a few days. Last night I saw Karl Kennedy, Izzy and Stuart from *Neighbours* in a pub. So I have a few good photos of me sharing a laugh with Dr K and friends. A few sad people started singing the theme tune, and someone told Karl to get back together with Susan. I don't think they realized he was actually an actor. Staying in some nasty hostel, and we are sharing a dorm with some strange Vietnamese guy who stares. Having a cool time.

It's quite amazing where you might brush shoulders with the stars. These two British girls go to a tiny township in New Zealand, and decide to go for a drink in the only place open, an almost empty pub. They fall into conversation with the barman.

✉ He asked if we were here to see the band – we saw a stage set up in the next room and three ageing African-American fellas stood by the door in sparkly jackets. We figured they must be the doormen, and when they asked if we were coming in we shrugged and said we would see what the

band were like first. At that moment the band were
announced: The Drifters! (As in 'Under the Boardwalk' and
'Sweets For My Sweet' and other classics.) Out walked the
'doormen' on to the stage. They were the Drifters! It's odd –
like a little bit of the 1960s has been sliced out and
superimposed on to this 21st century small-town yokels'
bar. As the Drifters shoop-shoop and do their funky thing, 6
or 7 locals dance badly and throw in the occasional whoop.

The band (it is highly unlikely that they included any of the
original Drifters, as led by soul legend Ben E. King) invite the
two ladies to spend the evening with them.

✉ It was a hell of a bizarre night. We ended up back at their
place watching videos at 5 in the morning. (We politely
declined the offer of a 5-way spar – we're not that rock and
roll.)

Next day they are invited to a champagne breakfast with
Wayne, Raymond and the other guy in the group.

✉ We finally staggered away about 4 in the afternoon. When
the check-out man in the local corner shop asked us if we'd
been at the Drifters' gig last night, the woman behind us
said, 'No, these girls partied WITH the Drifters last night.'
Small towns! It was time to leave.

Not all encounters with pop musicians are so agreeable. This
excitement occurred in Miraflores, Argentina.

✉ Casually strolling down a street we stumbled across a hundred screaming teenagers running after a car with blackened windows. After a quick enquiry we learned that it was an 'important' Argentinian boy band, so naturally, wanting to get in on the action, I made the hasty decision to climb up on Jerry's shoulders (for those of you who have the good fortune of being unacquainted with the dear old chap, I should mention here that he stands a formidable 6'5" tall). All was well and I could see as little as I could to begin with, when Jerry decided (slightly before I did) that it was time to get down. He moved forward. I moved back. You get the picture. The main attraction suddenly became me spaffing it from a great height on to the rather unforgiving tarmac. This apparently was enough to cheer up the majority of Miraflores for the rest of the day. (Something else I have noticed about South America is their love of the inappropriate. On our last long-haul bus we were subjected to a badly dubbed video of *Hannibal*, and while Anthony Hopkins was sawing through Ray Liotta's head and making Julianne Moore eat his brain, I noticed that 40% of the passengers were under the age of 8.)

Or this from rural Africa, an example of the wonderful way in which gappers' lives move from one surreal event to another in almost no time at all.

✉ Trying to save a buffalo. Think we'll get the vet in to tranc him. My horizons are certainly expanding. Going for dinner with some Germans tonight, a Baroness von Something and her third husband, who was thrown out of Argentina for slitting someone's throat. Or so I'm told.

Gappers learn about exciting new leisure activities, like this young woman in Peru.

✉ I headed to the Cusco bus station, clutching a load of luggage worthy of Joan Collins and aiming to go to Arica that night. However, got distracted and watched poor sods attempting to sandboard on the dunes. Sandboarding, I have come to believe, is the most pointless sport ever invented. The guys swagger up the hill with the board slung very uncomfortably over their shoulders, like milkmaids, they then stick the board on their feet, slide two yards, fall over, and watch in dismay as the board slides all the way down to the bottom, where the whole process starts again.

In China, they also make their own fun, as this young man working as a volunteer schoolteacher records.

✉ This weekend we had some ex-gap guys from Beijing and their friend from Vietnam. They arrived on Friday and I'd say the trouble started around the moment they unpacked their bags. They had been to a rather dodgy toy shop and managed to buy some of the sickest BB guns I've ever seen. They took us to the same shop and my Chinese friend asked, 'Do you sell any guns?' 'No, no, no, we don't have any.' 'Come on, we know you have.' Long pause. Bloke goes to storeroom, comes back with a bloody great box of guns and ammo, every type of airgun imaginable, shotguns, rifles, Uzis, it was so cool. We all bought one, and a huge sack of ammo. The Vietnam guy was hardcore, he bought a massive assault rifle and a laser sight as well as two handguns, 'just for spares'. At night we have the place to ourselves, so the stage was set for the ultimate BB battle. We even bought protective goggles because these guns could dent metal and break glass. The place was dark and with the goggles on you couldn't see shit. Our team, led by me, was moving slowly with stealth. I know the building inside out, and we took up an ambush point behind some classroom window. I was confident, then I look down and see the burning red dot of Guan Ming's laser sights ... ssshhhputt! ... the bastard opens fire, and soon we're on the run, his rifle is about 4 times as powerful as our puny handguns, and we forget that his people are famous for their guerrilla warfare skills. The shoot-outs were vicious, sometimes the bullets were breaking the skin. I got nailed in the face a few times, and one git even cracked my sunglasses. It was wicked, one of my favourite weekends yet, though next morning we were stuck with the problem of over 500 bullets to clear up. Better go and hide the guns, love, Rory

Gappers are no respecters of anything, least of all nature. This young man is in Bolivia.

⊠ Climbed the volcano, which was amazing, massive crater at the top, giving out smoke that hurt like hell when you breathe it in, had some great photos on the top of Jed having a piss, etc.

This girl says she is 'living the dream' in Sri Lanka, and it's easy to see why.

✉ We headed to a town called Unawatuna, awesome time. Won't bore you with the details, but I'll tell you this – had another rave, this time with a break-dancing midget, really freaky. He started break-dancing behind me and kept hitting my leg, so I started kicking his leg, as I thought he was some sleazy Lankan guy. Whoops! Have never laughed so much. If anyone wants anyone killed I can get my new best friend's dad to do it. I don't know what he's called, it's too hard to pronounce, so I call him Bob. He's 21 and ran towards the tsunami instead of away, apparently he wanted to see it more closely, and then he surfed. He's awesome. His dad is head of the Sri Lankan mafia, so a good friend to have, I think.

This young woman had a somewhat gentler time in Sri Lanka.

✉ I need to get down to the shops before everything closes down in anticipation of New Year's in a few days. Yes, my April birthday is on New Year's Day! I'm looking forward to it as two other volunteers who celebrated theirs here got presents from the nuns! One got a plastic paperweight with pictures of Jack and Rose from *Titanic* on the side, and mini-boats floating around inside. The other got a holographic picture of a house with plastic instead of a glass front, and set in a metal frame. I cannot begin to imagine what I'll get.

A gap year wouldn't be a gap year without a few moments of

pure terror. This young woman had a wonderful, and also deeply frightening time in Peru.

✉ We left Lima and within hours were wading through rivers of pure shite in order to get to the sea front in Pisco (where the shite itself was also heading), camped in wilderness in the most barren and dramatic setting I am ever likely to be in, flown in a four-seater plane over the Nazca lines while wondering why I was the only one who seemed slightly concerned by the way our pilot preferred to point out his favourite sand drawings using both his hands – that and the fact that the fuel gauge halfway into our trip read just below zero.

We camped on a beautiful beach and had a barbecue before a horribly tense bus journey against the clock because we had to cross into Arequipa before that night's blockade restarted! All was well, and apart from swerving around a few awkward middle-of-the-road fires and concrete breezeblocks, we arrived at the most fantastic hotel with en-suite bathrooms, high ceilings, balconies, sheets and bedside lights being the star attractions, and slept like logs on Night Nurse, stirring from sweet slumber only once when the earthquake struck. Panic not, mother, after the initial confusion I fell back to sleep straight away and woke up in the best of health, regardless of gaping cracks in the walls and pavements!

An exciting bus journey awaits us, where going on past experience we may entertain ourselves with impromptu mass karaoke and pub quizzes over PA system, including questions such as 'What is the average number of seeds on a sesame bun?' and 'What is the official word for a pubic wig?' More news to follow, hope you are well, don't do anything foolish.

There is something extraordinarily resilient about our gap-year students. This young woman is in Ecuador.

✉ I am nursing a particularly bad hangover, or 'chuchaqui' as they are called here, after a big night out yesterday where the whole group dressed up as either pimps or prostitutes and went to a restaurant where the cocktails were 99 cents each! Madness. I survived my weekend in the jungle. We took the bus from Quito to Nanegal, I had a man's crotch in my face for the entire journey, not pleasant. We then got in the back of a truck and drove as far up the mountain as we could, then started a long, very steep uphill trek to the place where we were staying, which was amazing. After arriving on Friday night, by Saturday afternoon the boys realized they were in need of fags, so they trekked all the way back down the mountain to the nearest shop, which is a 6-hour trek! They bought 7 packs of fags and a lot of booze, so the cloud forest was witness to quest madness.

On the Sunday we set off bright and early to the waterfall where we all got our kit off and swam in the freezing cold river, from then on we were wet through for the entire trip. As the heavens opened monsoon-style as we tried to get down to the bus, we needed a man with a machete to help us get through the jungle as there was a lot of debris on the path. We managed to get down eventually and then set off for Quito where we watched *The OC* on cable TV, such a contrast.

Tonight is 2 for 1 pizza night at Domino's, so I'll be staying in to recover from my one-too-many mojitos last night.

Doing something foolish is one of the principal reasons for taking a gap year. This chap, touring New Zealand, decides to go to the Hokitika Wild Foods festival. He winds up in a pub where he meets an English guy called Alex.

✉ It was quite a fun night. Those West Coast Kiwi girls are very forward and they seem to carry a kinda mad redneck vibe with them, which makes sense, as we are in the Wild West of New Zealand. So I get back to my backpackers' hostel, try to manage a bit of sleep beside the drunk, podgy and smelly Germans getting up for the bathroom every 10 minutes. In the morning I met up with Alex, stored my stuff in his car, and got going to the festival.

Hokitika Wild Foods festival is about drunk people trying all sorts of weird food mixed with lots of drinking and overall local Wild West fun where people dress up and cause general havoc in the town. Here is a list of what me and Alex ate:

Live Huhu grubs (had those twice, the second ones were much fresher, straight from the log)

Worm dhukka

Magpie pie

Raw eel

Ostrich sandwich

Eel spines

Fish eyes

Possum pie
Gorse flower scones
Horse
Crocodile
Kangaroo
Duck tongues
I think there's more but I can't remember.

This menu seemed impressive even at a festival of wild foods, and our gourmet gapper was swift to cash in.

✉ Here's the part where I become a celebrity. On the main stage the presenter guy called up people in the audience who've eaten more than 5 wild foods to go up there, Alex being too busy with a beer in each hand. I said what I'd eaten and where I was from, and everyone – and I mean everyone – cheered for me to get the free T-shirt. Then the guy asked me if I've eaten anything else, and I said I couldn't as I was running out of dosh, so he called out to the audience, 'Can we help this poor pommy backpacker out?' and so people started giving me money, I made about $60 – Oh! People were taking pictures of me in my T-shirt and if that wasn't enough fame the TV crew ran up to me and interviewed me for the Discovery Channel (I will be on TV in about 5 months, they said). So after my interview and a few free beers I also ended up with a place to stay in Wanganui. My legendary status lasted pretty much the rest of the day and bought me beers for the night. I was one happy Pom.

You have to admire this guy's guts, as well as his intestines. One senses that this email was more for the delight of his friends than for his parents.

✉ The next day I booked myself in to do the Thrillogy bungee jump offer, it's a lot of money but you get to do three different bungee jumps and you'll be pleased to know that I got them all on DVD for you to enjoy at home.

The first jump was off the Kawerau bridge, and it was quite a small one at 43 metres. You get put in a harness and then the bungee is tied around your ankles, while lots of Japanese take pictures of you. I was scared, I didn't scream in enjoyment. I didn't know I was screaming but apparently I let out a gut-wrenching scream which I've never heard myself do before.

Thinking the next one would be fine, it wasn't, I was crapping myself. The Nevis is 134 metres and you jump from a pod in the middle of a canyon. They do the usual strapping-you-up thing, but you have to shuffle on to this ledge like you're walking the plank, only hopping as your feet are tied. But boy, once I jumped, it was amazing, a brilliant free fall experience, so once I had the initial brickshitting, I let out many 'whoos' of enjoyment.

Now the third was a piece of cake, in this one the rope is attached to your waist and you can run and jump off and at 43 metres it was all over very quickly. However, I got to dangle for a while as I hadn't listened to the guy explaining the harness he uses to pull people up with, so I put it on wrong. You'll see all about that on the DVD, if I don't lose it.

Back in China, the fun just never ends.

⊠ Every year on 24 July Dali has fucking crazy fire day, all the
shop and café owners buy these big dried-out logs that
have been chopped up a bit so they burn well, and at
about 8.30 everyone lights up. Imagine a street looking like
some sort of road to hell with 10-foot pillars of fire blazing
everywhere. Then another sick element is added – wood
resin dust, you buy hefty kilo bags of the stuff, it's just white
powder, but when you throw a handful of it at one of the
flaming posts it bursts into a ball of fire … when people
walk past you they throw the dust and roast you. Everyone
wanted to burn me because I'm foreign, but Lucy got hit
the hardest. These two teenage lads saw her and threw
shitloads of that dust at her legs, she was only wearing hot
pants, so her bare legs were engulfed in thick fire. When I
saw this I ran and grabbed one of the lads by the throat
and started shouting at him in Chinese but I could hear
Lucy screaming so I had to leave him, giving him a push as
I walked away, shit, just thinking about it makes me furious,
if I find those kids I'll beat them to within an inch of their
lives. Can you imagine seeing people set fire to your
girlfriend? Lucy's legs are OK, she has them bandaged at
the minute …

A month later, and the couple seem to have recovered, though
they may be wearying of the country itself.

⊠ Me and Lucy went to see that bastard Mao's dead body this
morning, it's free to get in and they have him inside a big

glass room which you walk round the edge of, the armed guards won't let you stop walking so you get to see him for about 6 seconds, and he looks suspiciously plasticky and fake. If I have one thing to say about China, everything you see is fake, everything people say to you is a lie, at least that's how it feels on a shit day like this.

Others, like this young man, find China far more agreeable:

✉ The bloke who organized all our trips is also our friendly hash and ganga dealer, he kind of works for a local café, he's about 55, thin, and usually wears a badly fitting suit with a faded old sports cap. Yesterday we went round to Mr Xi's (Mr C) house. He lives with his entire family, including 95-year-old parents, in quite a big house with a central courtyard, the path leading up to his house was lined either side by small ganga plants, and he had a horse tied up by his kitchen door. We sat around drinking Chinese tea, then he gets out a mail sack full of ganga, and asks us if we want a pipe to smoke ('Cheers, Mr C!') and while we're doing that he puts on the end of *Titanic* on video and his entire family, around 12 people, gather round and we all sit there smoking weed and watching *Titanic*.

This young man, also in China, went to see his first ever football match.

✉ The match we went to see was the Chinese FA Cup final, Qingdao v. Dalian (I think). The final was split into two legs, and Qingdao had lost the first match 3–1 away from home, so we needed a 2–0 victory to win the cup. Now I've never been to a football match before, but this did seem a bit different from England, to start with everyone had these little plastic horns (yes, I bought one too) and when you're in a 60,000-seat stadium that's a lot of noise, but no one was wearing the team's colours, and they weren't really singing songs, although I did have some of the chants translated for me, one meant 'Step on the gas', and this guy behind me kept yelling stuff, apparently in English it meant 'I hope your mother dies', nice … the ref must have been taking the piss, because every decision was going our way, the other team even had a man sent off, and as he was walking off he was absolutely battered by bottles and oranges, I think someone even threw a shoe! Me and Tim started off a large part of the crowd waving goodbye to him, 'Cheerio, cheerio, cheerio', ha ha. The first half was 0–0, then Qingdao knocked in 2 in the last twenty minutes. The crowd got sick when the final whistle went, fireworks, drums, it was mental. Qingdao are the champions! I'm going for a curry later.

This young woman has been working as a journalist in West Africa.

⊠ Anyway, on Tuesday morning me and my co-journalist friend were sent to report on this political demonstration where thugs and hooligans were hired to cause mayhem. Spent all day trying to get on radio / TV / papers etc which wasn't very hard due to novelty of white skin. Pictures in papers of us holding signs saying 'Govt are theeves and

really shite' (signs forced upon us, spelling not the local
forte) and anyway they are trying to deport us. Completely
unfazed, due to newfound chilled-out persona.

Extreme weather is, of course, a source of great interest to
gappers. This is from Urumqui in northern China.

✉ On the way to Dunhuang we were in a sleeper bus for two
days. We had just spent two hours repairing a burst tyre
and had finally got back on the road, we decided to have a
game of cards, having watched the same desert scenery
endlessly rolling past, when everything suddenly turned
pitch black. We thought we must have entered a tunnel,
but in looking outside we were surprised to see we were still
on the open road. The sky suddenly turned from a murky
grey to a deep red, followed by a dirty, murky, raw sienna
colour and the bus began to shake and rattle from side to
side, we realized that we had been caught in a sandstorm.
We lay there in the bus as the sand lashed against the side
of the windows, twisting in the wind, forming wonderful
pirouetting sand devils that danced on the ground and
carried off anything that was not rooted firmly in the loose
desert soil. It may only have lasted five minutes, but when it
subsided we discovered that the sand had managed to
permeate the bus, our clothes, hair and even our teeth were
covered in a thin film of desert dust.

This young student spent a year in northern Russia improving
her language skills. The winter of 2005–6 was one of the coldest
ever recorded there.

✉ I know it is v dull to talk about the weather, but it is MINUS 30 degrees today, so I think I am allowed. All my shampoo on my shelf etc. freezes every night and children aren't allowed to go to school because they walk too slowly and tend to freeze to death before they get there. Nice. I am slightly worried as I walk at the speed of a lobotomized snail, there is 5 inches of ice on the roads and my new boots have strayed far from their natural habitat (the wilds of High St Ken.). On the first day of unbelievable iciness I happily stepped outside and within minutes my mascara had frozen my eyelids closed and my nostrils had iced over, after another few minutes I lost all feeling in my extremities, so by the time I reached the Institute I couldn't see, smell or feel. I walk so slowly that I am often overtaken by octogenarian babushkas shuffling along in felt slippers with massive sacks of turnips on their backs. Every day Ludmilla smugly informs me that it is another 10 degrees colder than the day before and happily tells me how to notice the first stages of frostbite.

But there is some good news amid the frost and snow.

✉ You will be glad to hear that I am hardly smoking at all, for I have managed to lose my gloves and as much as I want cigarettes I am unwilling to sacrifice any fingers to the habit. Luckily however for those times when I am overpowered by a craving for air which isn't horrifyingly icy, I have worked out an ingenious system where I hold a cigarette in a pair of tweezers with my hand in a sock. It took a while to perfect this system, as the first few times I either charred the sock or managed to get the tweezers frozen to my upper lip. But now I have perfected the art, and have the satisfaction of knowing I can defrost my lungs and look really cool, all at the same time.

With Friends Like These

One of the joys of a gap year is meeting other gap-year students. Well, sometimes it's a joy. It is when they turn out to be 'safe', 'wicked' or 'well fit'. It is less pleasing if they are wankers or minxes or mingers. Or 'gay', which these days is an all-purpose term of abuse. Sometimes painful people can be ditched and discarded, almost by the roadside. Sometimes, however, the gapper is stuck with them in the school or the building project where they are working. It can happen that the dear friend with whom you set off turns out, under the stress of travel, to be a wanker or gay, and is busily managing to ruin your trip. Or you encounter a mixture of all of those. The key word to bear in mind is 'annoying', the deadliest of the seven sins. This is from West Africa.

✉ I told some of you that what I was most worried about was not fancying any of the 38 boys that are here, well, that is an issue as I am most certainly fatter than them all and about as pale (one exception is the 18-stone boxer, but ...). I wrote this email yesterday but it got deleted and the boy sitting next to me read it, and so I had to drop subtle hints that he was the fittest (he is, incidentally) so it doubled up as cyber-flirting. I am progressing on the friends issue. My fellow volunteers have branded me 'the poshest person they have ever met', but apparently it was 'not meant in a "derogatorily" way'. Well, at least I don't make up words. Everyone is actually ace, give or take a few slightly annoying girls. I have taken to dropping my Ts when I speak and saying 'you ge' me' a lot. I also spend a lot of time talking about my stressful summer jobs etc. (Does Daddy getting me work, and Cowes Week count?)

This is from Peru and the young woman who sent it is working on a building project.

✉ Harrumph, slightly less grumpy today because dishy 'greenhouse expert' has asked me on a horse-riding date, but only slightly. Building project has escalated and I spent all morning shovelling cement, I shit you not, my arms will never recover. Builder's tan is now well established and I have made myself a brand new enemy, he is called Jed, and he is sooooo mean to me, don't quite know what course of action to take, might wee on his pillow and see how he likes it. My bogeys have turned black from all the mud and dust, my hands will never be clean again, and we have a snorer in the girls' dorm. Mike, the ex-marine, burst into tears at lunch because he misses his kids so much, and Kelly, the girl in the next bed, has ringworm, which by the way is highly contagious.

As for rules, we have a curfew at 10 and there is a no-drinking and no-petting rule in the home. Actually, quite like some of my fellow volunteers, so in all not bad, and am actually having fun, just a different sort from our usual fun.

This girl is teaching in Malawi.

✉ We are all finding it very hard to get on with Andrew, one of the boys living with us, who just seems to get more and more annoying, especially as he is now speaking with a South African accent, even to his parents, because he says he has picked it up (from where???!) and now can't get rid of it. AAARRRGGGHHH! Completely lost it with him the other night because he was being such a prat. Very unlike me, but he pushed me over the edge! Then Jan had a huge argument with him later that night, so a lot of tension between him and us, and now quite tricky because nobody wants to travel with him ...

This is from India, where ancient Hindu mysticism has yet to make its mark on our young Europeans.

✉ Went to the pub and saw all the other volunteers, who seem to be having a much crazier time than we are. After tomorrow it's only going to be me, Ellie and Drina in guesthouse, while the others are crammed full, so we will be completely out of the loop, and stupid Drina who is so annoying, and never sticks up for herself, and who has a stupid fake American accent even though she was only there a year, and has the HUGEST lisp and is doing her Masters in speech therapy – so all in all a complete nightmare, driving me and Ellie up the wall … off to have shower, but there's really no point as I constantly smell.

This is from a Catholic orphanage in Sri Lanka.

✉ Off to Trinco tomorrow and really looking forward to it. Just me and Em, because the other two are WEIRD. Nikki is from England and has a shaved head. Krissie is Canadian with lots of piercing, tattoos and seriously tight clothes. Both smoke like chimneys and the nuns hate them! Most of them want them out! It's been quite a drama. Em and me are saintly in comparison, and milking it.

Some fellow travellers can be quite interesting. This young woman has been touring Thailand.

✉ I'll describe some of the people I'm with. Hendrik and Nils – these two Danish guys we met in Chiang Mai and have seen every day for the last two weeks. Nils has a shaved head, and has recently learned the 'c' word, so uses it at every possible moment, and some you wouldn't believe possible. Hendrik dances like he's on acid, and he's not, I don't think, and he won't let you touch his Elvis-like hair. Both laugh at my (very) lame jokes, so I'm happy.

Jim, Kev and Jeff – these three boys (very generous word) we keep on seeing. Smoke opium the whole time, use words I never even knew – apparently unbelievably offensive – sing football songs constantly, get naked in every single bar, drink beer at breakfast, can't say a sentence without 'fuck' in it, jump into sewage water and make sure everyone is watching to see 'just how mental they are' and generally the kind of guy you would NEVER bring home to meet the rents, but would happily join with abroad.

Terry from Essex, forever smiling, half Indian and a bit fat, but very sweet. Sorry, shouldn't be fattist, but he is ever so slightly annoying, when he makes me look through all 750 of his photos from the last six months travelling. Eurghhh. But he is so nice I feel I have to be appreciative and make sure I use appropriate amounts of 'ooooh' and 'aaaah' and 'gosh, that's stunning', slightly loses its enthusiasm the 57th time.

There are many ways of being annoying. This lass spent time with tribespersons in Kenya.

✉ I made a goat curry and we sat around listening to Dolly Parton. The problem is they have only one tape, and it has about 3 songs on each side so I now know 6 Dolly Parton songs by heart. One of the guys from another base,

Bernard, was there that night, he is a born-again Christian, which was a little difficult. This guy sees visions of demons and stuff (or so he claims) and was preaching to us about the world being only 3,000 years old or something, and Piers and I were just being very quiet …

Or from a young woman who is teaching in a different part of Kenya.

✉ You will have heard about our school swap. Becca and I are quite glad because Antonia is extremely annoying. We first clashed with her when she announced, 'anyone can be taught English, but *Maths* is a gift'. She is doing a Maths degree, of course. The two girls we're now paired with are lovely, so don't worry, Mummy!

But they are not changing schools after all. In fact, matters become quite surprisingly complicated.

✉ Barry decided it would be much easier to swap two people – Antonia and Cassie – than four. Now Cassie is coming to our school. What happened was that Cassie met her partner and the other two girls she'll be sharing with at Heathrow, only to realize that one of the other pair, Yvette, was her worst enemy from school! Yvette felt the same way, so originally Becca and me were going to swap with Yvette and someone, but it's much simpler this way. So Becca and me are still at the same school but with Cassie, not Antonia.

Phew! Glad we've got that sorted out. But it matters –

companions really are important. This young man finds himself in Sydney, on his own.

✉ After a few hours' sleep I woke excited and expectant, hoping to see a hostel in full swing: people eating, cooking, chatting and doing other 'ings' besides. The reality, however, was very different. The majority of the backpacking community in Australia had moved north to Cairns, taking the party with it. Those that had been left behind were the human equivalent of the colour beige. They were boring spinsters and grouches who had come to Sydney months before with the intention of travelling up the east coast, but lacked the initiative to move more than 100 yards from the hostel, let alone buy a bus ticket out of Sydney. As a result many had ended up staying indefinitely and regarded any new people such as myself with muted suspicion and contempt.

Worse are people who attach themselves to you and won't take any hints about your wanting to be alone, or at least separated from them. This youth wrote from India.

✉ Oh news, I forgot, we bumped into Pete from Surbiton yesterday so we'll be travelling with him. Despite repeated attempts to poison her dates and put snakes in her bed, Deirdre from Manchester is still clinging to our bagstraps …

Travelling companions who turn out to be tossers are a serious problem. This is from Morocco.

✉ What an awesome last few days! Before I start I'd just like to say, Curt and I have kissed and made up, though he is still not coming to Crete. It's a damn hard thing travelling, it ain't all peaches and cream, so my words of wisdom are: be careful who you travel with, because even good mates can end up having huge blow-ups. I mean, it's only been three weeks. Me and Harry have got 7 months together, ha ha ha.

This can be a cause of some anxiety to parents at home. The following email arrived from Cambodia.

✉ Hi, Mumsie, I think you should stop being so lame and asking me if everyone is all right. Just cos I don't mention someone in an email (you know I only talk about myself, anyway) that doesn't mean we have had a massive fight and are not together, or whatever. We are having a seriously ace time, and getting on very well. So don't fret, pet.

This young woman has been working in a ski resort. As usual with gappers, work seems fairly low on the daily agenda.

✉ I have been blessed with two seriously entertaining flatmates. Peta is a 20-year-old who has a lot in common with Hagrid lookswise, who insists on watching me change, and calling me 'Treacle' at any given opportunity. She doesn't ski, all she does all day long is sit in bed and plough her way through copious amounts of chocolate, so I have made it my aim, albeit ambitious, to get her on the slopes if it kills me. Did I mention that she has got her hair down to

—

her bum which she only has time to wash once a week, cos both her and her flowing locks cannot fit into the bath all at once, so it becomes a bit of a mission. She spends on average 4 hours a day on the internet to her girlfriend who she has never met, and who is a trucker in America, quaint!!!!

Tracey: love her, she is a star, semi-professional boxer, keeps a knife by her bed, which, by the way, fell on to mine, the bunk below when I was out for the count. Her parents are publicans, and are coming to stay in a few weeks' time, so it's going to be cosy. Let's just say, kindred spirits are thin on the ground.

She sends a later update:

✉ I thought it was high time I gave you another insight into the quaint life I am leading. Masses has been going on. Tracey, my flatmate (the semi-professional boxer who keeps a knife by her bed) has been sent home. She toppled down the mountain the other day, got taken down by a bloody wagon, the driver of which was probably in a lot more pain than her, considering her generous curves. But the long and short of it is that I now find myself living with just Peta, the 20-year-old bisexual, dress size 22. I have, however, established that she does not see me 'in that way' so it's all quite chummy. I ply her with leftover brownies, which keeps her sweet.

My chalet is palatial, all the mod cons. In the past month the hot water has gone twice, the oven's broken, the bath doesn't run, the dishwasher is clogged and last week one of my guests came down the stairs looking somewhat pasty having been greeted by a mouse, sitting chilling by her bed. I was keen to keep it, my boss felt otherwise, and sucked the entire mouse population up with the Hoover. Brilliant.

My birthday was unforgettable. Four of my nine guests spent the whole evening chatting to the big white telephone and minutes before I was going to give the children high tea one of the boys chundered EVERYWHERE. Great party that evening, though, great party ...

Of course the first sight of the people you'll be travelling the planet with can be somewhat disconcerting. This is from Tel Aviv.

✉ Today we have spent hours and hours in the Indian Embassy dealing with our visa applications – I think they must make us hang around just to test how much we want to go to their country. However, we had a bit of light amusement as we waited, watching our fellow applicants, most of whom were aged, beardy hippies, or freaky-looking Israelis dressed in bug-eye glasses and strange attempts at traveller-type clothes, all of whom looked tough as the only form of nutrition they had had for the last few weeks came from a hash plant. Do you think these are the people who have found themselves? Slightly worrying ...

Drink, Drugs and
Rock 'n' Roll

What would conceivably be the point of a gap year in which a young person was not pissed, bladdered, mashed, smashed, wrecked, wasted, legless, and off his or her face for much of the time? As one young man points out in this chapter, faced with an offer of free beer, what is he supposed to say? No? Drugs, too, have always been an important if more worrying part of the gap-year experience. One curiosity is that since many gappers are the children of the first openly druggy generation – their parents tried LSD, many continue to smoke pot and some of the racier 'rents do coke – they are not particularly embarrassed about sharing their pharmaceutical experiences. Take this young man travelling with a friend in Thailand:

⊠ Parental warning: this episode does contain drugs, though sadly no sex and fortunately no violence. In the past episodes I have edited out my drug experiences for three reasons:
1. It has never been a core part of our travels, more a side issue.
2. You may be liberal, but it would be embarrassing to mention my drug experiences in front of my parents, and also I really dislike that drug pulp culture literature of Irvine Welsh and Howard Marks.
3. It would worry Mum, and everyone else. It's needless to mention unless I have an overdose, and I am sure you would hear from some means if that happened.

And with those comforting words, he gets down to a description of all the fun they have had in Thailand.

⊠ We headed for Farang village, full of crusties (who have not left since their LSD trip in 1974), also there are the ravers (coming up or down depending on the lunar cycle) and your average pedestrian tourist (following Lonely Planet religiously). I leave it to you to place us in a suitable category … anyhow the Full Moon [party] was at Bottle

Beach in the north of Koh Pha Ngan. At the first Full Moon I had a lot of expectations that were smashed by my motorbike crash, a dodgy mushroom shake and the fact that I could only hop. So going into this Full Moon I had no expectations, which is why it was so much fun. The beginning of the night was all blurred neon lights and distorted sound systems, me and Tom were reduced to meandering, wandering zombies through lack of interest rather than drug intake (don't worry, Mum!) …

They meet old school friends, which cheers them up, but not for long.

⊠ Anyway, calling the Full Moon party a 'rave' is giving it too much credit, I mean it is a huge amount of people dancing on the beach, off their tits, to poor sound systems, playing the same tunes again and again. Or maybe I am giving raves too much credit.

Life being a trifle on the tedious side, they try some magic mushroom omelettes.

⊠ My trip consisted of me imagining I was a 19th century sailor, also heard lots of music, the sea, trees, plants throbbed with colour and everything was really weird and fucking amazing at the same time.

Okay, maybe you haven't convinced us yet. Trips seem to be rather like other people's dreams – however fascinating they are to the person describing them, they are exceedingly dull for the rest of us. However, his friend Tom seems to have got better value for money.

✉ He thought he was a lizard, and created a reptile world. Looking back, what he describes sounds like rebirth, he re-experienced the wonder of his being. 'Look at my arm, I can stretch it, this is amazing.' I personally could feel the power coming from him, and it scared all three of us as he chased us into our bungalow. After his come-down, there were tears 'at our rejection of his new self', as he put it, though we all ran because he was tripping us out and chasing us. As soon as we heard him cry we looked after him, but he cried even more, saying he could 'feel the love we were giving him'.

They are not deterred, and three days later hit the omelettes once more.

✉ For Tom it did provide the next step. Instead of realization of himself, he had realization of the wonder of the world all around him. It was like he had re-arrived, constantly telling us how the world is round and it turns, and circles the sun – blatant stuff that confused me. After that he re-visited the morals he (and us) live our lives by, finally saying, 'love is the best thing I know, all you need is love'. He spoke this as if it was new, but it frustrated me that he thought it was new.

So nothing, you might imagine, could put young persons off drugs quicker than the experiences of the people who try them.

Rather than having posters showing brains being fried, or getting earnest policemen to visit schools, they could just have someone like Tom standing in front of the sixth form, mumbling incoherently that the world is round and all you need is love … Or this next young man could recount his experiences in New Zealand, narrated here in an email to – perhaps surprisingly – his mother.

✉ The local culture in Auckland is 'kandi'. It's a drug that is very similar to ecstasy, with one major exception – it's completely legal. I figured that as they were legal, they couldn't be that strong, so I ignored the warning not to exceed four pills per week and took twelve in one night. It was crazy. I forgot how old I was, and had to get a kid I had just met to tell me … about seven in the morning, the other guys tried to get some weed, and as if by magic a guy appeared out of nowhere offering weed. It normally wouldn't be a problem, but I was coming off the drugs in a serious way, and they are well known (to everyone but me) for their tendency to give people anxiety attacks when they begin to wear off. I was absolutely convinced that we were in the middle of a police sting operation and a squadron of police cars were going to come round the corner. I ran around Auckland for nearly two hours, freaking out. Every car seemed to have flashing police lights, till I got closer and could see it was a taxi. I even crossed the road from an old lady on her bike, just in case the police were using her as a decoy. I couldn't talk properly and my mouth was caked with dry saliva … it was the most screwed-up come-down I have ever had. Sorry it's been a few days since I last emailed, but I was convinced the police were checking my emails.

But the Kiwi police seem to be rather a helpful lot, at least to those who have not undergone a consciousness-lowering exercise like the previous young man. This young woman was with a carload of friends.

✉ We set off to Nimbin. When you read about this 'town' in Lonely Planet, it is described as not unlike Christiana in Copenhagen, a lawless community in Denmark where marijuana is sold and the police turn a blind eye to the activity provided it is kept under control and no problems arise from it. We were surprised to find nothing more than a tiny village, hamlet even, and everything was shut. So, tired and disappointed, we trudged into the pub. Emma had been driving for the 2½ hours, so I told her I'd drive back, and had a Coke. We then sat in the pub, clutching our handbags with varying terrified faces, until we realized that everyone was very friendly and not trying to make us into drug addicts. We asked the barman the quickest way home, and he wrote us directions, so we left Nimbin on the route we thought he had told us. Alice wanted to buy some marijuana, so had a quick chat with a man outside the pub, and a few minutes later had a small amount of locally grown weed. Then, 30 seconds out of the village, someone at the back pipes up, 'I thought we should have taken the other road, actually,' so I begin to execute a U, and as I do it, a police car pulls up alongside us. The policeman asks me if I've been drinking at all. I answer, 'No, just a Coke, is there a problem? Did I do something wrong?' He says, 'Yes, everything – only kidding! Just a routine breathalyzer, we saw you coming out of the pub.' (Did he see Alice buying weed? Apparently not.) So, the breathalyzer is clear, and I say, 'Ooh, I've never been pulled over before, can I get a photo of you and me together?' He laughs and thinks this is hilarious. 'Yeah, sure, now where are you girls going?' We tell him Byron Bay, we have these directions from the barman, do they look right to you? 'No,' he says, 'I don't know where he was sending you. Was he on drugs?'

Drug users have their own particular code of ethics, as revealed in this next missive from a young man in Bali, also to his mother.

✉ To put your mind at rest I haven't been tested, but if I was I'd be clean (that's the truth!!!). I've been offered marijuana tons and tons of times here so far, though. I could walk down the street and be offered it 5–6 times in five minutes. I've heard from people that it's literally just grass, however, the stuff off the ground! Also there are dealers around who work with the police and grass (!) buyers up and they have to pay a whacking great fine to be cleared. The dealers of course get their share from the police for setting up the situation. I don't think it's fair that there are drugs tests going on, people may have taken drugs before arriving in Bali, and still have it in their system, therefore it'd be none of the police's business.

Whereas, elsewhere in the Far East, obtaining drugs is less of a problem, as this young man reports.

✉ Greetings from Laos, 'Land of 1,000,000 elephants!' Laos
very rural and stunningly beautiful. So far we have explored
the north, which is deep jungle, hills, rivers and lush valleys
of bright green rice paddies. Laos is 40% animist tribal
minorities such as the Akkha, Hmong, Black T'Ai, White T'Ai
[possibly a joke] and they all wear amazing outfits,
headdresses, embroidered turbans and jewellery as everyday
wear, giving everything a kind of *National Geographic* look.
This takes a turn for the surreal when the old hill tribes
women, beautiful but toothless, pendulous breasts alfresco,
occasionally grab you by the arm, lightly pinching you and
tweaking you down to their level (4 foot). Then they glance
around in a deeply conspiratorial manner, whisper 'opi-u-u-
u-m' and give you a winning smile. Up here on the edge of
the Golden Triangle, opium is the opium of the masses.

Sometimes our gappers find that their druggy experiences are
actually a fine way of getting the chemicals out of their system.
This girl and her friend go to a 'Stardust Dance party' in the
Abel Tasman National Park in New Zealand.

✉ We spent most of the day watching people arrive and set
up tents, with an occasional walk around to see what was
going on. By about 8 p.m. they had music playing in all the
zones, but there were still not many people around. We sat
in the middle of the field in the sun, chatting to passers-by
and listening to the music. In New Zealand they have a
huge range of legal highs and Lex and I decided we would
buy some called 'The Big Grin'. It was a huge mistake. I
thought it would make us laugh, and we would have a fun

time, and that it would be safe because it was legal, but it made me really sick. I didn't take it until about 11.30 p.m. and had enjoyed my night until then, but was very, very poorly for the rest of the night … I am NEVER taking any drugs again, whether they are legal or not. I am really quite excited about this decision because I find that these days I do have the best time when I am totally sober and have all my senses at 100%. My body just cannot handle them any more, and the time has come to stop. FOR GOOD!!!!

In the end, in spite of all the chemical temptations, it does turn out that most gappers prefer good old-fashioned booze. Or possibly that's just what they want their parents to think. This is from a young woman in Peru.

✉ Thanks for all the birthday cards etc. I apparently had one of the best birthdays EVER! I would love to tell you all about it, but I haven't yet told myself! We went to McDonald's for my party, party hats and all! I was presented with a sarong and a bracelet bought by all the group, then we rushed back to watch *El Mundo No Bastar*, i.e. *The World Is Not Enough*, and played the Bond game. For those of you who don't know, this is where you have to drink a shot of a vile South American drink called Tropico every time the word 'Bond' is said in the film. Unless you have played this game before, it is impossible to believe how often they say it! After 11 times in half an hour, most people begin hoping that someone will simply shoot Mr Bond and be done with it, however by the end he is obviously still alive and well, and strangely enough you don't really care because you can't see the screen anyway.

Then we went out to Alfonso's bar. The birthday girl was still the centre of attention (still wearing her Ronald McDonald hat, and now also streamers from somewhere). All the group plus loads of random people bought drinks for her, bastards. Lots of dancing on the bar … then someone gave me Bob. Bob is a very special coin, but he cannot swim. If he 'accidentally' falls into your glass then you must, without hesitation or breathing, drink all of it in order to save him. Despite virtually swallowing him I did save him from countless deaths but he never seemed to learn and strangely seemed to prefer my glass to anyone else's, bastards again.

Sometimes drink serves to blot out the more displeasing parts of the gap-year experience. This young woman is in India:

✉ Having slight problems roughing it; stayed in Banglampoo last weekend and spent the whole of Sunday at the Taj Hotel at their brunch – all-you-can-eat, all-you-can-drink – and lounging by the pool, not exactly budgeting, and then two days ago had a wax / hair / facial / manicure/pedicure thing at the hotel!!!!! But, come on, it's not that bad, is it? Actually did feel slightly embarrassed when one little man was doing my feet, another my nails, another my hair. Slight low point when they commented that I really should get my arms waxed, and while we're at it, what about that moustache, and then proceeded to ask if I had a boyfriend. I try not to read into those little comments. Valentine's Day came and went extremely unmemorably due to cheap, rank vodka, and lack of any form of mixer, resulting in projectile vomit everywhere – silly, silly me. But I try to look at the plus side, and tell everyone that at least I had someone to prop my head out of the sick bowl, even if it was only pale Ginger Jim.

Alcohol of course can land people in situations they would rather not be in. Take this girl, in Laos.

✉ Being the absolute lamo that I am I can't seem to handle drugs and so have had a lot of self-consolation, while my companions wander, actually probably fly, into Happy Land. Went tubing for the first time a couple of days ago, all great. You stop at these bars on the sides of the river and have 'Beer Lao', etc. etc., and then there are these swings which hurt your arms and are petrifying (yup, fell off mine very early in front of huge crowd and sympathetic half-smiles) and the ants that bite you, so you have little red marks all over your chafed, red-burnt skin, but anyway, we took ages getting down the river, having far too much fun, and it suddenly got really dark, so, all the others got out and got a tuk-tuk home, me and Chloe decided to grab on to these two kayaks and get rowed to the end. My rowers were Albion and Joe. Both with dreadlocks, tattoos, perma-spliffs lodged in their mouths and bloodshot eyes. I thought, what an adventure! We soon lost Chloe and her men, so I was all alone with my new friends, in the pitch black, on a river, and suddenly flashes of light and rumbling thunder turned my adrenalin-crazed excitement to serious fear. Literally would have cried if I hadn't been trying to be hardcore in front of Alby and Joe. (Can you believe he was really called Albion?) But, basically, huge thunderstorm, we ran aground millions of times, and got so stuck they nearly had to leave me behind. But I tricked them into thinking I was a vicar's daughter and did he know what would happen to him at the pearly gates?

Got home eventually, Chloe waiting for me, all was fine, next morning we woke up and did it all again.

As the Communist Party loosens its grip on the new China, alcohol appears to be flowing in to take its place in the affections of the masses, as this young man records.

✉ Thursday night was Da Yun's birthday, so he had a private party in the bar, and guess who got invited – yes, me and Baz. We had a wicked free supper (tasty grilled chicken and posh herby mashed potatoes, with two tiger prawns on top, yum) and they brought out the huge birthday cake and things started getting messy. I think it began with people playfully dabbing bits of cake on each other's noses, then Laurent upped the stakes and squished about 1/4 of the cake into Da Yun's face, pretty soon everyone there was spatting cake around and this escalated into beer being thrown, people getting drenched and after not too long everyone was just filling up jugs with water and properly soaking each other, everyone was so wet that clothes started coming off, mainly the ladies! Even I spent most of the night with no top on. Easily the best party I've ever been to. I'm going to go so far as to say it was the best day of my life so far.

A few months later absolutely nothing has changed for our hero.

✉ Hi Jeff and dad! Thanx for all the birthday dosh, should keep me drunk for the next couple of weeks. Tonight me, Jen, and all the teachers are going to Jimmy's bar for a meal, which Jimmy is putting on free of charge including loads of free beer. Then we'll be going to the French bar to drink sangria until we pass out. Last night me and Sean built a beer bong, we bought a length of plastic tube and a funnel. The funnel is attached to the end of the tube, and basically you fill the thing with beer, hold your thumb over the end of the tube and the beer shoots out into your mouth. Drinking this way you can down a whole large bottle of beer in about 12 seconds. We got pretty drunk last night.

Not everyone's experience with booze is quite so agreeable. This young man was in Greece.

✉ My last night in Crete was easily the most eventful. I went down to the local shop to buy some souvenirs and see my friend Phil. There were two Americans there, also buying stuff, and we started chatting about this Cretan drink called raki. So Phil pulls out some for us and we start drinking this vodka-like drink, which is absolutely potent. Then he brings out apples, cheese, bread and carrots and we have a mini-dinner, extremely nice and enjoyable and the raki goes a long way, hee hee hee. So I finally head on back to the hotel around 8ish as I have an early start to catch the plane tomorrow – once again Americans were helping me by

—
45

giving me a lift to the airport at 5 in the morning. When I get to the hotel another American, different one again, offers me a beer, so we start chatting and drinking, he's buying me free beer, what am I supposed to do? Say no??? Then he mentions ouzo, and I'd never tried it, so we start having a few shots of that.

The result is, perhaps, inevitable.

✉ Needless to say, next day I slept in, missed the wake-up call, had to run down the huge hill with my pack to catch a bus to the airport that would arrive too late anyway. Luckily a taxi came and he hit 160 mph to get me to the airport on time. I think I left my stomach in Chersonisos.

But this was a mere inconvenience compared to the experience suffered by a young woman in Australia.

✉ Am now back at Sydney airport, wait, I'll rewind. Went and stayed with my and Lizzie's friend Sophie last night, got smashed beyond belief. Then have blackout till I wake at 6 a.m. this morning and realize I have missed my flight and there is sick all down me, and I have broken a rib, don't ask how or why or what happened as I have no idea. Walk out of the house and get into a taxi, still wasted. The madness continued when I tried to argue my way on to the flight, it still wasn't taking off for half an hour. When you're drunk and have sick stains all over you and smell like a baby's nappy it doesn't help. They gave me the option of getting another flight tomorrow and only paying $70 or getting the next one out and paying $400. I get the expensive flight that leaves in a while. Then I stumble through the airport, having been chased for not paying the sodding departure tax and got milked of another $25. Asked if I was 'all right' and told to get a move on. Angry. Very angry.

You will not be surprised to learn that things just get worse.

⊠ Buy four bottles of water and get on the plane, very plush, turns out I'd just paid for bloody business class. People next to me, two wankerish Germans, start holding their noses and laughing at me, to my face, only a blind man would not have realized they were laughing at me, smelling of sick and the white stain on my jeans. I then pass out and wake up for the last 10 minutes of the Harry Potter movie. I love Harry Potter and now I know the ending. Arseholes.

Am now at Sydney airport, trying to remember where I left the car. I think I will probably die, in which case I love you lots.

But this young man suffers more than seems fair for one small, drunken escapade.

⊠ Life here in Thailand took an unexpected turn 4 days before Christmas when I got into the festive spirit a little too early, and got a little too drunk, and thought it was a good idea to jump over the wall at the back of my house. I found myself with blood dripping down my arm at 3 in the morning, trapped in someone else's backyard. I inexplicably knocked on the window leaving a massive smear of blood and understandably terrorising the neighbours. I summoned my last strength and hauled myself over the ten-foot wall and into the safety of my own house. Less than ten minutes later, we heard a knock at the door, to my horror it was a complete platoon of policemen.

He is hauled off to the police station, along with his two friends and housemates. He is then thrown into a cell with ten other prisoners.

✉ The next day came and went and I was starting to get extremely worried. When Jack visited the next day he told me that encroaching on someone's property was considered a very serious offence in Thailand. Disorientated and disillusioned, I stumbled back to the foul, damp, gloomy cell that could be my home for Christmas and the New Year. The blankets were more hole than blanket, and the floor was splintering. In the corner was a communal loo. I hadn't showered, and was beginning to smell and was desperate for a shit I couldn't bear to take. I didn't sleep too well that night.

Next day five of us were cuffed together and taken to a much bigger cell with 30 other criminals, all wearing luminous uniform and with chains around their legs. I was eventually told that we had been taken to a courthouse and were to be sentenced, probably for 12 days, to stay either in the police station (I dreaded that thought) or pay bail of 50,000 baht, which meant telling my parents and asking them for £750. It didn't look good on any front.

He is duly sentenced to twelve days and goes back to the police station. His friends visit less and less often.

✉ Christmas Day came and I had only the visit from Jack and Rog to look forward to. It never came. Hour after hour dragged on and still nothing. Visiting hours were over and a herd of carol singers reinforced the devastation of the worst Christmas ever. That night I prayed and prayed. I'm no great believer in God, but that night I prayed as though my life depended on it.

The prayers are answered. He is visited by a Briton called Arthur, a Christian who tells him that the victims of his trespass work for his wife.

✉ He asked, was I sorry for my actions? Tearfully I answered 'yes'. He had brought me a KFC and I was overwhelmed by his generosity.

That is a rare recorded instance of someone being relieved to be handed a box of the Colonel's special secret recipe chicken. The fairy godfather tells our hero that bail will be £450, and since it's a Bank Holiday in the UK, and his parents can't get the money to him, offers to lend it.

✉ A couple of hours later they released me into the sunlight where Arthur and his wife took me home. It seems I won't even get a criminal record, all because a stranger who had never met me, stepped in and did everything in his power to help. I am eternally grateful.

—

Love, Romance and Just Plain Shagging

For our gappers, love is almost always in the air. It might be with a fellow student, or with a dark-eyed stranger met in a jungle clearing, or it might involve someone living in a culture totally and exotically different from that of Petersfield or Solihull. There are two reasons why a traveller might wish to describe adventures in the glades of Eros: to boast to friends back home, and – just as important – to wind up unsuspecting and fearful parents. It is in the nature of such matters that one can never be quite sure what is going on: whether the events described actually took place, or are wildly exaggerated, or are simply imagined in the gapper's mind as he or she sits on the beach, round the campfire, or passes a dull moment in the staff room. Take this email from Africa, which back in the Home Counties must have caused a few cups of Gold Blend to shake in their saucers.

✉ Hey, mum: met a chief of a neighbouring town on Thursday and so I started babbling away about new rough skirt and drastic haircut, etc. It suddenly dawned on me that he was a 'talk only when spoken to' kind of guy. So embarrassing. He's actually really nice, thirty-five, seven wives, and apparently looking for an eighth … Hope all fab, love Jan.

Surely this one is a wind-up.

✉ Dear Mummy and Daddy, how are you? This may come as a shock but I am thinking of eloping with one of my students to Assam coz he is from the Naga tribe, and I want to be a Naga girl and go hunting monkeys with bows and arrows and fishing with spears like they do, and then come back and do tribal dancing all night, coz it's so much fun, and all the tribal people here are so great and brave and strong. Obviously the political situation in Assam isn't ideal, but I'll be OK, love you lots. Only an idea at the moment. X, Me

With this one it is hard to be certain, but it does echo the theme of our book.

✉ Those of you who remember my obsession with Boyzone will be pleased to know that I have at last accepted that it was not in fact Love. Yes, there were fireworks, aching heart, longing, scary dreams, posters etc., but Wantoto is SO much more. He is so strong and macho and puts Ronan to shame. Also, he can do far cooler dancing around the fire. Have told him to come back and live with us in England. Not sure how Mum will deal with it – I know she will love him, though. Mike, you are absolutely NOT to tell her yet. I am going to call and discuss next week. Lots of love, Rose.

Local customs can create confusion.

✉ Hi Mum, did our concert last night, the press and TV were there, even though it was rubbish! We played cricket for over an hour this morning, without a bat, ball or stumps. It's really amazing! One Indian boy asked me to escort him and later asked for marriage. Didn't realize that walking with someone and talking to them for more than a minute is the go-ahead! Must go, lots and lots of love, X

And courting customs can vary from one continent to another. This is from South America.

✉ The girls I am working with all have internet buddies. One of them is called Fabrizio and has one of those rough rat's

tail things at the back of his head, and as if that wasn't
gross enough, he tried to get me to plait it for him, at
which point I no longer had any understanding of the
Spanish language and ran for the hills. He also plays piano
and insisted on playing every Beatles song under the sun
and singing at the same time. Well, I have tried to avoid
using any Spanish words in here – always find that a bit
gay.

'Gay', of course, being used in its new sense of 'not good,
embarrassing, misguided'.

It has to be said that wistful regret is the principal tone of
many romantic emails, combined with a wish to reassure
anxious parents that nothing has transpired that might require
expensive medical attention. The following email is also from
Latin America.

✉ To all concerned: I should tell you of my recent loss – 'fit
Dan' has parted from us for pastures Bolivian and I feel
deserted and empty. Jo is doubtful of our connection. Just
to clarify, over two weeks the 'relationship' proceeded as far
as: a single conversation, a blown kiss after my birthday and
a comment on my 'funky' trousers. But there was a whole
load of bubbling eroticism and sparks, and now I don't
know how to cope ...

Some relationships do seem to have been doomed from the start.
This is from a young woman working in Malawi.

✉ I am in love!!!! His name is Patrick, however unfortunately he has a girlfriend, and he flew to Australia yesterday. (He is also a little bit on the short side for me, but you can't be that picky!!!)

And there is a world of mild sadness in this message from Laos.

✉ Life is pretty swell, everyone we meet is doing the same trail as us, so we keep bumping into our fellow travellers at each new place, which is quite fun. Although it does make the long bus journeys ever so slightly embarrassing, when you end up sitting next to someone who has photos of you from the night before, table dancing in our bikinis, and playing 'truth or dare' – typical dare – 'go up to that person in the red T-shirt and tell him you've been watching him all night and that you think it's love, blah blah blah'. It invariably has negative consequences, as you (a) get stuck with them all night and miss everyone else's dares, or (b) they laugh in your face and you go bright red – thanks for that, by the way, Mum, the redness – or (c) they say, 'well that's all very nice, but you're not really my type,' which is rubbish, coz it's crap not being someone else's type, however little you like them.

This is from West Africa, where work for the poor of the developing world is interspersed with more pressing concerns.

✉ My exciting news in a nutshell. (1) On my birthday (well remembered, some of you, and for those who didn't, I thought that mentioning it in 3 emails would be enough), two people snogged and the girl was sick in mid-kiss, all over the guy. (2) Two girls are having a massive bitch fight over this other guy. Little do they know that he doesn't like either of them. Petsy is fit, so I'm not sure why he is not keen, but Leah, her rival, is ever so slightly annoying. (3) Everybody keeps telling this Irish guy I really fancy him, which I don't by the way, so now he blushes every time I talk to him, and I'm like 'why?' so now I don't talk to him. Shame, cos he's quite funny.

This email from the beaches of Sydney was probably not meant for parental eyes.

✉ No action yet, but I'm working on it, problem is that there is rather a lot of hot crumpet around to compete with, and they can surf and I can't, and they are skinny and I'm not.

Even when they do get some 'action', it doesn't seem to extend very far. Or at least the writers don't admit it. This is from a young man just back from Greece, writing to a friend who is in Malaysia.

✉ Well, I got back from sunny Kos to wet Scotland. With a dyed blond mop! Mum was not impressed and I had to shave most of it off!! So now I have short blond hair and ginger eyebrows, and look like a poof. So there's not much difference! Bagged myself two girls out in Kos, don't actually know what they looked like, but we had some good tonsil tennis before parting ways.

This leads him to some homespun philosophizing.

✉ Love is like an egg, it can be hard and difficult to overcome, or it can be soft and easily broken!!!

Or, to extend the metaphor, never comes out of the shell. This student is doing a professional cookery course for her gap year.

✉ Got a new mission to occupy my evenings for the next 2 weeks. Was in the pub on Sunday, and in walks one of our friends, Steve + 1. The +1 happens to be called Parker, and is drop-dead gorgeous. I mean really, really fit. Sooooo, I can't really speak, and decide to flirt with Sam in our typical flirty relationship. Parker is well quiet and sitting on my other side. So I break the ice, we chat a bit, all going pretty well, but he is quite shy and sweet, and I realize that it's love, with the big L. Anyway, I quickly think up plan to get him to our house, so invite them all swimming and for after-pub drinks etc. It all seems great, he's really keen. About an hour later, we're now quite close, but I'm being really subtle, thinking I have loads of time to charm him … but him and Steve say they have to go and have supper, but maybe see us later. When they've left, it's just me and Joe and Sam, so we go swimming. I then explain my new infatuation, and they are shocked, and tell me he's a wanker, and all this stuff. I finally get them to explain why, it's because he shags all the fit women …

A delicate touch at the end there, worthy of Jane Austen. The email then becomes what psychologists call a cry for help.

✉ Question is: I have been to his pub twice, which is

—

57

apparently where he hangs out, but can't quite think of the necessary excuse to stop off at his workplace. I drastically need your help. So reply NOW! Joe says that the fact that he is called Parker is enough for me not to fancy him. Jamie says I will just get hurt. But I know I can change him ...

Yes, dear, of course you can. And one day Jade Goody will rewrite the theory of relativity. Luckily this young woman has an older sister, who replies with wise counsel.

✉ Not sure what to say about your dilemma. I think it is a bit much to stalk him, only very rarely are stalkers successful in their attack, and usually it is through sleuth [stealth?] and anonymity in their pursuit, so the subject does not realize he is being stalked. I fear, even from thousands of miles away, that you may not be the subtlest of pursuers. What does he do? Could you visit him at work, let out a gasp of surprise along with 'Do you work here? Didn't I meet you the other day? I just came in for some stamps, novelty masks, double glazing etc.'
   Personally I think you should leave it, but then we are very different people, and as long as you don't call your children Parker, it's up to you. Maybe you could persuade everyone and their +1s to come for a supper party then give the wrong day to all others except this guy and, I suppose, his introducing friend, lock irritating friend in the loo with some stuffed vine leaves and with an 'Oh, look, we're all alone!' exclamation proceed to show him your tattoo. (And get some henna, I have a feeling it may last longer than this relationship.)

After a while you get a feeling that sexual disappointment is built into the gap-year system. This young man had been touring around South-East Asia, and was on his way to Australia.

⊠ There is something about being on a plane that completely alters the way I view myself. I begin to think that I am irresistible to women. This train of thought begins in the check-in lounge as a twinge of self-confidence around the opposite sex, and gradually increases on the walk on to the plane. By the time I am in my seat and belted in, this twinge will have mutated into the all-out delusion that I am an instrument, sent down from heaven by God himself, for women to be charmed by and attracted to. I have no idea what causes this chemical reaction, though I did once think that cocaine may have been passed through the air vents, though this seems a touch far-fetched. Thus, on the flight to Sydney, it was with a head oversized with self-assurance that I began chatting with the woman next to me – a fairly hot 26-year-old in advertising.

Every movement she made, and every word she said, confirmed in my drugged mind that my irrepressible 19-year-old charm was working on her and she was coming on to me. Before long, was envisaging a sordid, 3-day affair at her trendy pad in central Sydney. However, these castles in the air that I had been building since take-off – by this point each came with servants, 16th century tapestries and a working portcullis – crumbled and fell when she mentioned she had a boyfriend.

Not all was lost, though, as she promised to give me a free lift to the youth hostel.

Sometimes a tone of near desperation sneaks in. This is from email-land, somewhere in Africa.

✉ It's my birthday tomorrow and I am making everyone dress up. All very unimpressed. I made the mistake of suggesting chavs. At least everyone would have a costume. Unappreciative silence, so quickly changed that to African, and so am wearing a flag as a dress. (Very short, and see-through, as am fed up with this no-action stuff.)

Going travelling this weekend with 5 boys. Am making everyone share one bed under the false pretence that it's budgeting. It's actually because I can't not pull if there are five of them. Can I? (That was a joke, in case you didn't get the sarcasm. I am *not* a slut.)

Of course not, dear, what could have given us that idea?

✉ Valentine's Day was mental. Roger, fat boxer guy and potential date, feigned illness so he wouldn't have to go with me. Apparently he is scared of my 'perpetual enthusiasm and hyperactivity'. I didn't know he knew what those words meant. It wasn't as if I was going to lunge. Anyhow, my nice friend Dan became my date and all was rosy. Not literally, obviously, because Ghana doesn't do anything classy, think more glittery, popping out cards, and plasticky teddies / fluffy hair ties.

It could be worse. She could be in the middle of the Australian outback, like this poor lass.

✉ I definitely couldn't live out here, it seems like a very lonely life, especially after Sydney, and the fact that I am living with two reserved grown-ups and two kids under nine doesn't help to spice things up. The slight saviour is the Irish farmhand, he has just left uni, and is farming out here for three months. However, when I first saw him in the swimming pool yesterday he seemed to find me very embarrassing and blushed every time I spoke to him.

I definitely wouldn't describe him as a conversationalist and have to say that he is about as interesting as mud, but at least I can go and talk at him when I'm bored, it's brilliant because he doesn't interrupt any of my fascinating stories ... am going to the beach this weekend, but won't venture into the sea as there have been quite a few shark attacks recently and don't really like the idea of being eaten. Tibby, very proud of your skydiving and snogging achievements ...

This young woman is also in Australia, but seems to have fallen in with some New Zealanders who are rather more articulate than the Irish farmhand.

✉ All the boys went to an all-day rave on New Year's Day, but I'm afraid that I am far too sweet and innocent for that, and went to the beach, it was 44 degrees, hottest day in 50 years, and I managed to get burned through my Factor 60 sunblock, and now look like Rudolph with a red peeling nose. Two nights ago the Kiwi boys took us to King's Cross, which is the seedy, gross part of Sydney, and took us to a strip bar, never seen anything so disgraceful in my life. The boys bought a lap dance and watched while a naked girl writhed all over us, playing with her boobies and fanny. I didn't know where to look, all highly embarrassing. She had had her clit pierced, which was rather interesting. When we asked her about it she said that it hurt to get it done, but has improved her sex life by 200%, so there we go, girlies. Must dash, have to go to the supermarket to buy some yoghurt, don't get me started on the yoghurt, it's unbelievably amazing.

As I say, gappers always find a consolation, even if it is only yoghurt. The next, not entirely dissimilar, experience came from a new graduate who took a gap year in Thailand after his course had finished. He writes in a deliberately mannered style, as twenty-two-year-olds sometimes do.

✉ Upon achieving an advanced state of over-refreshment, we settled on the idea of venturing to Patpong Road [Bangkok], thinking to see some of the fine night market there. After arriving we somehow ended up in an establishment called Super Pussy, a form of cabaret or vaudeville featuring several young women in various states of disrobement, demonstrating some of the extraordinary tool-using abilities of the female genitalia. Shocked by this vulgarity we could only stay for an hour or so, before heading in the direction of more genteel entertainment. Sadly, it appeared that every club on this road was full of the same villainous thing, in most cases of a higher quality and with more becoming performers. Upon the hour of midnight, with our pockets quite empty …

Going to clubs can be a mistake, especially when they turn out to be brothels. This young man was touring Argentina with his girlfriend. She had lost a game of Jenga, and her forfeit was to buy drinks. Which meant going somewhere where drinks could be bought.

✉ Enforcing Susi's Jenga punishment had always been unlikely, however somehow at some time after midnight we found ourselves a little tipsy in a taxi heading towards the village and the seediest dive in town. I could write forever about that fateful night, but I'll cut it short. Basically we ended up in a place called Rouge, where 50-year-old American businessmen go to receive what they can't get at home. We were completely out of place, and when we got the bill found ourselves completely out of pocket. My first piece of gap-year advice: if you ever find yourself in a dirty club after a drunken game of Jenga, remember that when you buy a drink in one of these facilities, you are in fact buying time. So it is kind of expensive. And the proprietors of these establishments aren't very nice, when we told them we didn't have the money, we were threatened with the police again. Then they wanted our watches, so we paid up. At the end the owner had the balls to put his arm around me and asked me when I was returning.

Yes, you'd think that gappers would realize by now that clubs in foreign lands are always, almost without exception, a bad idea. When it comes to a fine evening's entertainment, a good book and a milky drink are a much better idea. This younger woman was in Queensland.

—

✉ Night began, me and Hat sitting at the bar, when this fit guy comes over and asks if we'll do the podium competition for 8 free drinks, me trying to flirt, giggle and say 'of course'. Why not? 8 free drinks. Don't know really what I was thinking of as didn't even know what a podium was, but anyway persuaded Hat to do it, reluctantly. We both forgot about it and carried on drinking away when suddenly everyone is ushered into this one room. As I walk in I suddenly realize what a podium is when I see this cage in the middle of the room, 10 feet in the air, with a dirty slapper dancing topless in the middle of it, grinding against the side. Next thing I know, my name is being called and I am climbing up this ladder on to this tiny platform. Help!

Men cheering, music begins, me frozen, giggling, looking around, Hat on the floor in hysterical giggles and saying 'copy me' as she dances away. I start, stop, giggle, look around to all the men (about 300) with their hands out, thumbs pointing down, saying 'booooo'. Makes me laugh even more … I swear it was the longest minute of my life. What made it worse was that Hat then got up and shook her boobs and won the competition, so I had to walk around with this goddess all night and men giving me the 'what WERE you thinking?' look. I swear I will never enter a podium competition again.

Over in China, some chaps had more positive experiences. This boy is also travelling with his girlfriend, who seems to be an adaptable type of person.

✉ We went to a bar called the Bird Bar, inside an old building, it's very dark with low sofas everywhere. It's a bit hippy, but kind of cool, last night everyone was wasted and dancing, the only light in the place came from candles, in a dark sweaty atmosphere people started losing their inhibitions. It started when a cool 18-year-old Chinese hippy babe took her top off, she was dancing around with her tits out, pretty soon a lot of the guys had taken off their tops … I went out to roll a spliff, then I went back inside. I wasn't ready for what I saw. Everyone in the bar had taken some clothes off, every girl had her tits out, and about three possibly Korean girls and the 18-year-old hottie were just dancing in their thongs. I would like to say now that I am officially not lying.

It was maybe the most fucked-up night I have ever had, the bar turned into some drum and bass orgy, almost naked fit Asian girls were dancing with me, and when Billie saw how interested the 18-year-old minx was in me she immediately took her top off and got up to dance, at one point I was sandwiched between a fit Korean girl in a thong and Billie. I don't mean this to sound like I'm boasting or making up bullshit, the girls out here love foreigners, and since all the other guys were about thirty-something geeky-looking hikers, they fucking loved the English guy with the spiky hair. Later on I went to take a piss, the toilet only has bamboo screens for doors, so I'm there taking a leak, when a fit Chinese woman bursts in, she was obviously wasted, and without saying anything she leans over (I still have my todger out at this point, though I have finished pissing) and kisses me on the lips, then she spots me glancing at her chest, so she cups one tit in each hand, and jiggles them sexily, then disappears. Thinking back to last night this

morning, it seems like a weird hedonistic dream, not what I
had come to expect from Chinese people at all ...

I'll say. The eternal wisdom of Confucius may not have
penetrated to some rural areas. Or, as the old joke has it: 'British
man: Shall we try some 69? Chinese woman: I'm not cooking
for you at this time of night ...'

Another young man in China had a calmer, charming
experience. He had been introduced to a twenty-year-old
Chinese girl who had excellent English.

⊠ I may as well tell you that I seriously fancy this girl, she's
funny, gorgeous, and she speaks with this sexy London /
Chinese accent. She came to the Hallowe'en party on
Thursday, and ended up sleeping in my bed ... no, nothing
like that, I was sleeping on the floor like a gentleman. Next
day I went with her to get my hair cut, and just as we were
about to leave she looks at me with her beautiful Chinese
eyes and says 'So, do you want me to give you a kiss?'
Hmmm, let me think ... so she leans forward and kisses me
on the lips, and just stands there smiling. I think I'm in love.

He is even more smitten when he discovers that in her part-time
work as a tour guide she gets very bored.

⊠ So she makes up things to tell the tourists. In fact, she's
always lying about everything, but it's just funny because
her lies are so stupid, e.g. 'You know, in the south of China
they train very small pandas to work in restaurants, they

bring the food to you on a little tray tied to their heads.' Me
and her get on great.

Back to Thailand, where many strange things happen, especially
to young girls:

✉ Went to the Half Moon party, which was absolutely
shockingly bad, really bad! Lots of trance music, which was
too loud, and quite crap. The day afterwards I was having
my lunch, and there were three people who looked really
worried. One of the girls' boyfriends hadn't come back; at 2
he turned up and it was like Eastenders, live and for free. He
had been drugged and lost all memory, but woke up in a
hut with a ladyboy, love bites and all his money stolen! And
now an ex-girlfriend – pretty harsh but really quite amusing!

Thailand also seems to quiver with sexual ambiguity. These
three British girls decide to go for a massage.

✉ It works out at about £3 for an hour. We went in for a full
body oil massage and headed upstairs to a spooky little
room. There was no turning back now. Sara bravely said
she'd have the Thai man, and we thought we'd be safe with
the women. We were wrong. We lay side by side and even
had some banter with the women. It was all lovely until my
lady flipped me over, got my breasts out, and started
vigorously massaging them. I was a little shocked to say the
least, and didn't have much say in it. Jacqui looked over and
said 'Jesus!', and then I started to laugh. The lady said, 'Oh,
you're not shy, are you?' and I just lay there shocked. Then

—

she did my back, and I was violated once more when she went on to my bum. She kept slapping it in a strange way, and saying 'Oooh, lovely …' The others had normal massages with no violations, but I guess it's all character-building. Hope the sun is shining in the UK.

Misunderstandings can come from the simplest of causes.

✉ Went to the market [in Africa] and got given a strappy top advertising a new internet company. On the front it says 'fast, cheap and easy'. So I decided the donor must have been well into irony. My friend got given one saying 'friends are forever, boys are whatever', surely it's better to look like a tart than a lesbian …

Or misunderstandings can be created deliberately. This is from a young man who is about to leave Greece and go home.

✉ One last weird story before I leave you all. In the airport in Athens I began talking to this Lebanese guy. He told me that he travelled a lot due to his job. I asked him what he did, and he said: 'Oh, my friend, this is an amazing opportunity for you. You can become rich and travel, if you work with me and my friends.'

I started getting worried that he was going to plant a drug-trafficking assignment on me, but it turns out that he was a wacko trying to force a pyramid-selling scheme on me. He was crazy. He kept telling me how he liked me deeply and could tell I had dreams and ambitions. Then he started touching my leg with his pen and drawing circles on my knee. It was then that I rushed a hurried goodbye. However, he caught me in an embrace before I could get out and kissed me on the ear. I ran like hell. WHAT A WEIRDO????? Anyway, I return to mundane life working in a pub in England.

Perhaps the most unfair thing that can happen to a gapper is to be treated for a sexual disease without actually having had sex. This is from a girl touring India.

✉ Mummy, just went to the doctor's again, and the nice man told me to take some pills, so I did, and have just looked on the internet and found that they are for 'unexplained swelling of the scrotum after sex', but don't worry, I did some more research and they are also for bacterial infections etc. If you could check for me with Dr Hutchins if this is okay, I have been told to take one 500mg tablet of Aziwok (for my scrotum) once a day an hour before breakfast for 3 days, then one tablet of Voveran SR 75 twice a day for three days after food. Am really worried about this scrotum business because I didn't think I had one. Still missing you x x x

Take This Job
and Shove It

Some gappers are lucky and have parents who pay for their travels. Others have to earn the money. One way of doing this is by taking a job, frequently in an office. The attempt to get early experience of an ineffably tedious future in the world of work is often a mistake. This young woman, saving for a world trip, contacted her sister in desperation.

⊠ Am seriously in need of help. I have to type up this letter and email it to some joker in Newcastle within the next half hour. There are only three minor problems:

    (1) it is audio typing and the guy has a REALLY strong Geordie accent.

    (2) there is no spell-check on the programme, so I never knew that Newcastle had places as exotic-sounding as 'Glennorrrayyend' which has featured at least 7 times so far.

    (3) I have just deleted the audio so now can't even check what I have done so far and have to send it.

Two and a half hours later:

⊠ Okay, so … Just emailed that audio-typed email (all wrong but I figured something was better than nothing) TO THE WRONG PERSON. My sent items automatically delete and I don't have the audio message to do it again, due to aforementioned spastic error on my part. The MD, who I was doing it for, has gone back to Newcastle now, so, shall I just not tell anyone? Am leaving in two days. I'm slightly concerned that it was marked 'PRIVATE' and I sent it to the other property agent, the rival company. Remind me, when I am a highly successful businesswoman, to NEVER hire incompetent temps. I am officially rubbish.

But of course businesses never learn. Usually it's because the temp is the daughter of a good friend or business contact, and they are happy to do him – and her – a favour. This is generally a mistake.

✉ HELP HELP HELP. I just shredded some documents that I was meant to file, and filed the ones I was meant to shred. HHHHEEEELLLLLPPPP!!!! Fu*k, Fu*k, Fu*k. Fu*k. I can't even take out the ones I filed, cos I can't remember which ones were which. Shall I email the bank and get them to send the documents through again? I am not sure my flirting is up to them not telling my boss. Suggestions please. My happiness, and therefore your happiness, depends on me keeping this job. All love, a desperate and soon to be unemployed Jessica.

This girl got a job in a London department store.

✉ Hey, all, you're probably wondering why I am emailing midday. Well, I have been sent home from the shop, after an embarrassing but mildly funny morning. Got so plastered at Baz's bar last night that while I was serving a customer this morning in the home section, I could feel those little drips of water inside my mouth which are a forewarning of the imminent hangover vomiting session. Yes, I smiled at the customer facing me over the till, and ran out of my section, and promptly spewed all over the floor of the next-door showroom. My boss immediately assumed I was coming down with the flu and sympathetically sent me home. So here I am, relaxing at home, preparing myself for the Tropicana tonight. And I didn't even have to clear it up! See you all tonight.

One can only admire the magnificent way our students feel the need to recover from a hangover purely in order to prepare for

—

the next hangover. This young man, however, appears to have had a less exciting time.

✉ If you don't already know, I am in the lush and verdant pastures of sun-drenched Aberdeen, deep within the tropical paradise that is north-east Scotland. I work with a large multinational engineering company, who love throwing big lumps of metal into the North Sea to suck up the oil from underneath. It's all very entertaining. I make a mean cup of coffee and can now photocopy blindfold standing on my hands using only my two big toes. My colleagues are about as fun as an unexploded party popper, i.e. I would rather be just about anywhere on earth.

Others go into teaching, which frequently ends in tears. This young man went back to his old prep school.

✉ I hate little boys. I hate little boys. I hate little boys. I hate little boys. I hate little boys. [This rubric is repeated 27 times.] Why, when I was so desperate to leave when I was 13, was I ever persuaded to return to my prep school, and tuck the little runts into bed, at the exploited rate of 62p an hour? Matt kindly told them I am gay, which, if you remember days at prep school, was the ultimate insult, but I also seem to recall one was a 'gaylord' if you were last in the classroom, missed a goal in football, or for pretty much anything.

Nevertheless it's not so great because they complained to the headmaster that they don't want me to go back to do their lights because 'Jeremy is a gay'. I got back on Matt by

telling the dysfunctional little psychos that he had a
girlfriend, which apparently is far worse than being gay.
Half-term next week. Whooooo-peeeeeee!

Another serious mistake is to become a chalet girl. Few people
do this twice. They go out imagining a relaxing few weeks spent
with like souls sharing quarters in a lovely mountainous area. A
little light housework and cooking will be followed by a day on
the piste and a night on the piss. This is sometimes, but rarely,
the case.

⊠ Guys, I'm back from Courchevel. Got fired, my boss was a
wanker. Anyway, women were shite and I can't be arsed
cooking for ungrateful guests. Never go on a 'Ski-mania'
holiday. They are all tossers. Does anyone have a job for
me?

This young woman went to Val d'Isère.

⊠ I'm looking after a nine-man chalet and as a result I've done
75 hours' work in the last four days, they are squeezing
every last drop out of me, but things are looking up
because I think my guests this week are giving me a massive
tip. Quite right too. Nightmare, though, cos I've got two
veggies staying and have managed to give them
minestrone soup made with chicken stock, which they
lapped up, completely oblivious, in raptures, then last night
they were less amused when I whacked a plate of jelly in
front of them, I soooo nearly told them to get stuffed, but
bit my tongue, just.

—

Last night one of the guests was complaining that she had the runs, and I had to break it to her that the company had run out of loo roll. Day off today, so she's been without for 24 hours! Not pretty when cleaning the loo tomorrow morning.

This is also from France.

✉ I am the most shit chalet girl ever. The idiot I was working with left me and fucked off as I'm apparently too laid back, so have had to cook for 12 people all by myself, which has been a disaster, and this gap-year malarkey has made any brain cells I did have completely disappear, so I made a cake using olive oil, which tasted more like Mediterranean salad and which I left in the oven too long, so I had to cut about 5cm off the edge, which made it more of a cupcake, gave everyone red wine diluted with white wine instead of kir, which was undrinkable, and then forgot to put any baking powder in my scones so they burned in the oven and looked more like little piles of poo. Then I had to remake my mince pies as they all stuck in the pan (yes, you have to grease the little bastards), which was a bugger.

Have had the most awful guests this week – a whole lot of peasants who think they're really great. I overheard them bitching about me the other day, which just made my day, and they keep shouting at the table, fuck off halfway through supper and grumble that the food is cold, complaining about everything including the fact that their breakfasts didn't come out all at the same time, so they had to wait, the fact that I won't make them lunch; and next week have a whole load of rich French and Italian guys who are turning up with their hookers, which should be interesting, but will get an enormous tip.

The excitement of having free / cheap drinks has meant that I have had only 2 nights in since I've been here, so now I have lost my voice, which doesn't even sound cool and husky but more like a 13-year-old schoolboy or according to the rep, a telephone sex hotline, and look like a wreck after no sleep. Have also managed to wreck a pair of seriously nice skis, which have now been binned as I lost control completely and bombed down a steep run without turning over all these rocks. Apart from that it's loads of fun.

Mistakes made, horrible people encountered, but money safely tucked away, our gappers head off for their spell abroad. Many do voluntary work, and the most common occupation is teaching. This can be a joy and a delight – and a useful learning experience too.

✉ Life in Sri Lanka seems to be getting better every week. Love working here, partly because the students are older so give me no sh*t and secondly because they all worship me, as I'm a volunteer, here to save them. So my mission to save the world is going quite well. The orphans are so cool, I was told one of the cutest boy's story, and cried … his dad killed his mum by cutting her leg off then beating her in front of him and his 5 brothers and one sister. He is only 12 and this was 4 years ago. Love him. The boys at the orphanage are amazing. They don't understand yet what we're saying, so when we play Pictionary it's a little difficult. Have decided to kidnap one of them, he's 8 and called Kalum, cutest boy ever in the whole wide world. I adopted him when we had to go to the school sports day. Had to don a sari for the day, my, my, my, have never been so hot, maybe won't be doing that again in a hurry. It's awesome though! Everyone loved it that we made an effort, so we were the centre of attention, which was annoying as no one watched the sport, but we loved it!

This fairly catastrophic event took place in Malawi.

✉ Had sports day yesterday which was sooooooooo stressful as we all went out the night before and had to boil 60 eggs for the egg-and-spoon race and do all the score sheets very early in the morning, but all the students loved it. We got so sunburnt and then Jack and I had to walk to the market to get supper for everyone in the torrential rain, so we also got very cold and wet – weird sensation! Then, just to top it off, we realized that we had lost the sports day results, so had to kind of make them up.

This young woman in Kenya accompanies her pupils to an inter-school music competition:

✉ Next to the other schools, our primary children look like a Kenyan version of the Bash Street Kids. The neatness of the other competitors only made us more fiercely loyal to our little darlings, and the music teacher, Mr Wafula, said that we sounded like a hundred people cheering rather than three. I was also filled with maternal pride when they came second, a feeling which surprised me as I spend most of my lessons confiscating ingenious catapults made from a hollow biro and an elastic band, unsticking small children from the wall in art lessons, or avoiding eagerly offered snotty hands.

They are also getting bolder and wander into the house without warning. This means it's not unusual to come out of the bedroom wearing nothing but a towel to find three small children in the kitchen trying to take apart the gas stove. I'm doing reading lessons to help a 4-year-old called Tracey, and it's going well. You may think that Tracey is an odd Kenyan name, but I teach Wayne, Brenda, Maureen, Kelvin, Brian and Eric. I'm also helping with a national art competition, although I had to explain to Mr Okingo that 'helping' was not the same as 'doing 20 entries myself and getting the children to write their names at the bottom', which is what he wanted me to do.

If those names sound curious, they are as nothing compared to those this young woman encounters in Malawi.

✉ Teaching is getting better and better and my class are all so adorable. (Really want to bring them home with me!) Teaching them sport is also amazing as they are all so eager, because they don't do sport unless the volunteers take it. Played Stick-in-the-mud and British Bulldog for a bit of fun and the boys were literally diving under each other's legs and wiping each other out while others were looking up the girls' skirts! We have had to abandon any form of dodgeball with the kiddies as it becomes so violent, so we are playing lots of netball, volleyball and rounders instead. The English teacher returned yesterday after being ill for a week, but he is seriously pervy so Luce and I are avoiding him at all costs. Got my first marriage proposal yesterday from a boy student in the top form called 'Precious'! Having a real issue with all their names, like 'Computer', 'Warehouse', our night guard is called 'Diamond Cabbage' but especially with a girl in my class called 'Labia' – very hard to keep a straight face when talking to her!

On Monday Luce and I taught our first proper PE lesson so we put on our shorts which actually aren't that short as far as shorts go, and couldn't understand why the entire school just stood still and stared! Turns out that if you bare your knees by wearing shorts you are a prostitute, so they went quickly back into our bags!

Sports can be a hazard, as this young woman found in South America.

✉ Well, day two of Spanish school in Guatemala and wasn't really sure of the form, so in an effort not to seem aloof and too British signed Ness and me up for all activities. Ness and I are now playing in a friendly football match with our fellow pupils against the teachers this afternoon. Never really played football before, but have watched it on TV, although that approach hasn't always worked in the past – see home decorating.

The job is not always agreeable. This is from southern India.

✉ First day of teaching today, they don't understand anything and all we are meant to teach them is the alphabet, and how to pronounce it – so, incredibly dull and it's only one-on-one so not even a real class. Anyhow, trying to keep positive about it, but am finding it hard as all I did this afternoon was make a poster with wild animals drawn on it – I have now found my talent in life of making children's posters but all my animals looked pregnant and seriously deformed, but never mind.

Eventually booked somewhere for this weekend with me, Jan, Maeve (now a regret, as she is a nightmare) and Hamish, so random cos saw him for like an hour and he said 'just book me with whatever you're doing' and haven't told him since, and we are going tomorrow night and spending 12 hours in non-air-conditioned bus all the way to Goa. Basically it's all trial and error.

This is from a school in India.

✉ Teaching is interesting and to a certain extent rewarding, except the children are reminiscent of the devil and the teachers have the same warmth towards us as an Arctic glacier. I have taken to teaching my children the most useful things they need to know about English culture – last week we learned about Sloanes, pikeys, Geordies, wide boys and lager louts. I have become the chief slayer of insects, having combated cockroaches in my sleeping bag, wash bag, pants, loo seat, hairbrush, as well as taking on a spider the size of a small elephant. I am indestructible! – though the dysentery wasn't great. Had a nasty run-in with a leper carrying a python this morning, but being invincible, and the worldly girl I have come to be, I took him on. I am now slightly worried how contagious leprosy is. Hope you are all well and disease-free.

Some placements can be quite horrible, such as this one in Tanzania, where the young female teacher meets a Third World Wackford Squeers.

✉ I only have another 5 weeks in the school – v. sad but on the other hand, can't wait. The school is run by an Indian man and his family, and he is possibly the biggest s**t that has ever graced the planet. He was in India for the first 6 weeks of our time here, thank God, but the month or so we have had with him has been horrid. Yesterday he repeatedly kicked a 6-year-old for making too much noise (the boy has loads of scars all over his face, so evidently has a pretty tough time at home). He smashed two 5-year-olds' heads together and threw desks around in the direction of the children. I walked into the classroom just after this had happened and I have never seen children look so scared. Luckily I had them for next recreation, so took them outside and played. The worst thing was that the children were all kicking each other and fighting more than usual, obviously as a result of what they had just seen.

Here is a classic instance of a gapper, in Malawi, finding comfort and consolation in the midst of trying circumstances:

✉ I made a big boo-boo in the staff room last week. We were

all chatting and I said 'cheeky little monkey', referring to a really cute but naughty student, only to find the whole room had stopped in horror, thinking I was being really racist! Managed to laugh it off but won't be making that mistake again! Very sad also as the brother of one of the teachers died and another's wife died during labour this week, I think the funerals are next week. On a cheerier note, had a very hectic weekend as all 22 volunteers came to stay at our house to celebrate T's birthday! Had to cook sausages for everyone in the smallest saucepan I have ever seen, but with all the delicious Malawian gin and vodka (not!!) no one seemed to mind the long delay, or the fact that they had to sleep on the stone floor.

I'm on a Gap Year –
Get Me Out of Here!

The whole point of a gap year is for youngsters to keep their eyes and minds – and their nostrils – open to new experiences. Unfortunately they often don't greatly care for the new experiences. Many people simply want to be home again. Generally, it is in the earliest part of the gapper's trip that he or she is likely to be most homesick. Arriving in a strange and alien place, without family or friends, knowing this is your life for the next few weeks or months, can be one of the bleakest experiences a young person can have. This girl wound up in Shanghai.

✉ Couldn't find driver at airport for ages, but eventually got here. Seriously dingy apartment in an equally dingy-at-best, grim-at-worst part of downtown west Shanghai. The school have given me a bedroom with peeling paper, then tried to glam it up with a new fridge, toaster, TV (all strange Chinese dancers and business news) and water machine – water not drinkable … roads filled with drivers exactly like me, perhaps worse, people rely on fate over indicators, signs or eyes to transmit their destination. Nearly got run over by a Chinese lady on a moped piled high with boxes – got yelled at for ages. Noise of traffic everywhere – bedroom filled with it. Smells disgusting.

This message from Bangalore was even more glum. India can be very disconcerting to someone arriving for the first time.

✉ I know you will say 'stick with it, it has only been a week', but believe me when you come to this armpit of a city you will understand my predicament. Yesterday we had to find something to do, so we went to the 'bustling city market' which turned out to be yet more fly-ridden fruit stands and a few stalls selling those hat things that Sikhs wear, why they thought I as an 18-year-old English girl would want one I have no idea, so abandoned that idea and read that there was the 'highlight of Bangalore's palaces' (yet another excellent reference from Lonely Planet – which I want to burn), so looked for about a squillion minutes and eventually found it. I had to pay 100 rupees, whereas the locals only have to pay two, talk about prejudice, and managed to find one thing to comment on: it was symmetrical. Great. Kath and me are planning our escape, which I still think is imminent – may be able to stick it out for another few weeks, but another 7 – you have got to be joking.

A hundred rupees is only around £1.20, so it's not so awful. But the experience might have been bearable were the food worth eating. After all, most of us can work through a grisly day if we know there will be some pleasant browsing and sluicing at the end. Not in Bangalore, it appears.

✉ A miracle did occur yesterday evening when we were actually given something else apart from rice, dal and chapatti, some noodle things and some potato stuff, because I think if I see another lentil in my life I might well vomit, or more likely turn into one.

Others learn to cope with India. This is from a young man.

✉ Several things have changed since I arrived. I think I've lost about a stone, and I've learned to be a veggie. What else? I can sleep through all imaginable nightly disturbances and contort myself into a ball whenever I need a quick nap, sitting up in a public place. I am able to move between extremes of wealth and poverty without shock, and I can

wind up a window when there is a child begging for money
outside my taxi. I can fix a broken rickshaw, cross a deadly
intersection, and keep from gasping when the driver hits
the brakes to prevent us from hitting a cow. I am oblivious
to the sound of car horns. When a street vendor takes my
money and doesn't give me change, I can yell until he does.
The same goes for people who take my train or bus seat. I
have learned how to squat over a hole and simultaneously
puke on my feet. I now know how to eat with my hands
just after I wiped my ass with them. I have learned that you
can get bored with Indian food ...

Some people just can't hack it. This poor lass found West Africa
especially hard to cope with.

✉ Dear Mummy and Daddy,
The streets of Cape Coast are littered by night with the
bodies of children and entire families trying to sleep under
the street lights with the background noise of bars and
drunken brawls. I have never seen anything like it. Even at
my hotel there are people sleeping on the steps because
they have nowhere else to go. Bodies inhabit every edge of
pavement. It is truly harrowing and terrible. Miss you all
lots, sorry this is so depressing.

Likewise, this is from Thailand.

✉ Having seen *The Beach* I thought Phuket was the place
called 'paradise'. However, when we docked, we were
literally horrified. It is the most commercialized, touristy,

noisy, smelly, busy, tacky place ever. The locals have
surrendered their island to tourism, but I guess they have
little choice. It is so depressing.

Sometimes the most famous backpacker novel can paint a more
beguiling picture than reality, sometimes not. Either way you
have to admire the pluck shown by this girl and her friend.

⊠ Two Swedish girls told us they knew of a hostel that was
'basic but really cheap', so feeling grateful for any help, we
followed them to El Carretero, which is the rank below
Hospadaje, which is the rank below Hostel. Basically it was
exactly like *The Beach*, filled with weed-smoking wannabe
Rastas and words of wisdom (e.g. 'Dung Beetles Must Argue
A Lot') and skeletons scrawled on the walls. We were rather
gleefully informed that the dark stains in the corner were
blood. Determined to look like we were used to this kind of
hardcore-shit-man, we smiled dazedly and signed in. We'll
see how it goes, Debs

Crime is a constant nagging worry for gappers, and for those
they have left behind. This email would not have brought much
comfort to the writer's parents.

⊠ Well, I got mugged again, trying to get across eight lines of
traffic from Cinelandia to the Modern Art Museum in the
pouring rain. He did have a knife, but he wasn't particularly
threatening, and he let me open my wallet and give him
the notes, rather than taking everything, which would have
been a pain. It's okay. I'm used to it now.

Gappers can even laugh in the face of crime.

✉ Having defeated a bizarre, orange-outfitted local at a
dance-off on the Vietnam clubbing scene and celebrated
with a couple of kebabs, I got a moto taxi home where,
having felt extremely smug with my curls blowing in the
wind, when I opened my wallet to pay him he snitched
200,000 dong (the equivalent to what a teacher gets paid
in a month) from my wallet. Although this seems a lot of
money, it's only 7 quid, so I found myself giggling at his
boldness!

Or maintain a stiff upper lip, as in this missive from Ecuador.

✉ We have also got to cheer up this English bloke we met on
the Inca train, and who we met again today in Quito. We
were moaning about bus journeys, but he had it much
worse on his way to Ecuador from Peru. His bus got held up
in the middle of the night. Apparently the bus stopped
(nothing unusual about that) and a bloke got on with a
police jumper on but also wearing a balaclava and holding
a gun. At first he wasn't sure if it was a passport check but
that thought soon went when a couple more blokes with
guns got on and started shouting 'Money, money' in
Spanish. Then everyone was robbed of all their stuff at
gunpoint ... he didn't have any money as he'd cunningly
hidden it behind the curtain and the banditos didn't believe
he didn't have any money so they made him drop his
trousers and checked his pants. Luckily for Perry he had $25
in his pockets, so they just took that and his watch,

although everyone later realized that there were three more
bandits outside who emptied the luggage hold. He did have
his travellers' cheques, his passport, ticket home and his
camera, which was under the seat, so it could have been
slightly worse.

It's not just Europeans who meet perils. This message is from
Shanghai.

⊠ Getting back to the hostel, I thought it would be fun to try
and assemble a new set of drinking buddies, so I got talking
to the other lads in our room, an Aussie called Mel, he
seemed pretty safe, and a cool Japanese 'clubbing maniac'
called Norio. It turned out that a couple of nights ago a sly
Chinese temptress had drugged poor Norio while he was in
a club. 'I am feeling very dizzy in my head, bitter tastes in
my fruit drink, then I wake up in hotel, she take my phone,
my money, everything. Be careful of Chinese women, they
are very clever.'

But some gappers can manage to find reasons to get depressed
wherever they are in the world.

⊠ Chile is so different to Peru. At first I loved the tackiness and
the Western atmosphere. I couldn't talk for about ten
minutes when we discovered a McDonald's, but after about
three hours it all started to pall slightly. It was all so
expensive and not even amazing ice cream could make up
for the feeling of being in Birmingham.

Even Australia can be disappointing. This young man is not unhappy so much as gently rueful.

✉ In all that time I had nurtured an idea of Sydney, where streets overflowed with bikini-clad women, surfers and yuppies, whose bronzed bodies reflected the sun's golden rays. So when I found it was in fact wet, cold and overcast, I was pretty damn annoyed. 'But at least there will still be beautiful people,' I consoled myself. I took a right down into King's Cross and any life that still existed in my idyll was smothered.

For those that don't already know, King's Cross is Sydney's red-light district and it is completely delightful. The beautiful people I had imagined were replaced by dirty, fat old men, pimps, the occasional crack whore, and some of the weirdest people I have ever seen. It was not uncommon to see one, two or even three tramps talking, or more commonly shouting, at an imaginary friend. One of them did a fantastic rendition of *'Roxanne'*, with the aid of a bottle of whisky and a busted microphone. He gave the song an individual and, I think, rather special touch.

So the first four days passed by in a miserable, grey whirl of stifled conversations with boring and pretentious travellers, some as interesting as *Newsnight Review*, early nights, poor food and shopping. Apparently dirty cargo shorts and shrunken fake designer T-shirts are not as much in vogue in Oz as they are in Asia.

Rescue comes, as it sometimes does, from family friends, who happen to have one of the most glamorous apartments in

Sydney, and life takes a sudden turn for the better.

If Australia might occasionally be a let-down, less advanced countries can cause something closer to real alarm, as this young woman discovered.

✉ I will not waste time talking shite, and will tell you some extremely useful and insightful facts about Venezuela:
   1. the women like to wear tight tops. Even if they are fat.
   2. the Venezuelans appreciate little rat-sized dogs.
   3. there are no Venezuelan cats (to my knowledge).
   4. some taxi drivers enjoy watching (intently) a small portable television taped to their dashboard while driving petrified tourists through dangerous streets at night. This is not fun.
   By now you must feel like you're here yourselves!

One of the main problems faced by gappers is needing medical help in a foreign country. This traveller is in Thailand.

✉ I have spent today in hospital, as three of us have abscesses on our feet from getting 3cm of glass stuck. I kid you not when I say they just shoved the needle straight in, and then proceeded to pick out every grain of sand from the seven cuts. This is when I realized how hardcore everyone is here, as apparently people rarely complain. Errrr, whatever. It was, quite simply, the worst hour (yes, it took a whole hour) of my life. I seem to be saying that a lot, but don't get me wrong, I absolutely love this place, bar the glass, and the police who have busted lots of my friends with various

—

substances, the heartless / ruthless / satanic nurses –
obviously the people who stole my other friends' cameras,
money, the losers who stole my clothes when I went for a
swim in the early hours of this morning, and of course those
pill-heads who I met one night, and one is now stalking me,
but other than that, all is well.

Drugs of a medical nature can also be a constant source of
confusion.

⊠ We are now west of Delhi. Anxiety very much rose during
our trip to the desert, as of course risk of malaria and rabies
was greater. Lucky – they were the two menaces I was least
protected against, the rabies jab I didn't have enough
money for, and malaria tablets I had to skimp on by getting
the cheapest ones. Rabies was not an issue in the end,
because the dogs were moth-eaten specimens of filth with
about as much charm as Gary Glitter. Rabies aside, I was
reassured by the presence of malaria tablets in my bag –
that is, until I read the usage guidelines. I do not know if
anyone else is using Doxycycline but (and I promise you)
there is no mention of malaria prevention on the box. It
simply reads: 'antibiotics for the fast and effective relief of
gonorrhoea and other fungal-based STDs.' Lesson learned –
never skimp on necessities. I'm buggered. However, looking
on the bright side, they might come in handy after a
romantic evening …

But things could be quite a lot worse, as this young woman
discovered in Peru.

⊠ Just a quick note that will hopefully act as a deterrent to anyone planning on getting ill, particularly if you are in South America. Went to the hospital yesterday, and following a physical examination by the doctor, which involved getting topless in front of two highly over-excited midgets who were repairing the wall of the surgery, I was then told I had to have an injection. All well and good. However, this part of the operation took place in a small shed overlooking the main road, and it is apparently against medical practice to close the door. I stood for five long minutes with half the human and animal population of Urubamba looking on, as a doctor filled the syringe, pulled my trousers down and leisurely injected about a gallon of fluid into my lily-white arse … hope this has put you off, lots of love, xxxx

The Third World is not always kind to skin. Away from the soft rain of England and the moisturising creams of Estée Lauder it can quickly come to resemble a half-prepared building site.

⊠ We have managed to discover a secluded beach on a very dodgy island. Some very nice Thai fishermen took us here. We are not convinced of their intentions, however, or indeed how likely malaria and dengue fever are. I'm not exaggerating when I say I look like I have acne and my body feels like I'm the victim of a very serious burns incident. I really hate bugs actually. Eurgh. Also I really hate the torrential rain that is hindering (to put it very mildly) our sleep. Secluded beaches aren't quite as exciting as I thought. But they do have internet and no loos … bizarre.

—

It must be terrifying when you, or one of your friends, find yourself in urgent need of a hospital in a Third World country. Especially when you have very little money. This young woman, travelling in India with two friends, spent a horrifying few days.

✉ On Friday M started getting ill again. She stayed in bed the whole of Saturday, just sleeping the whole day, wholly unconsciously. On Sunday morning she started being violently sick, even though she hadn't been able to eat anything the day before. She couldn't even keep water down, so we decided we needed a doctor ...

So begins an experience that might have brought a wry smile to the face of Franz Kafka. She goes to a phone box to call the insurance company, who ask her to fax them the policy, then runs back to the hotel which has undertaken to find a hospital, but the 'moron' manning reception claims to be too busy and disappears upstairs. After ninety minutes she finds a hospital which will send the bills direct to the insurance company, but she hasn't got a taxi. They try to phone for one but nobody will send one, so she goes into the street to look, finds a cab, asks the driver to come in twenty minutes, somehow gets her friend downstairs to wait – and they wait, and wait, and wait. She walks to the taxi stand ten minutes away.

✉ I eventually get a taxi, it drives me back, we pick up M, after 10 minutes into the journey I realize I've forgotten her passport. We eventually get to the hospital 20 minutes later and they rush us into Emergency. They say they'll admit her, but nothing about the insurance guarantee. I rush around the corner to use the phone to ring the insurance company, they say they'll ring the hospital again, except the hotel I'm ringing from won't give me a number for them to ring, and the receptionist won't talk to the woman on the phone, so I ring back in 10 minutes, they say the hospital should be all prepared and I rush back to the hospital, find M in tears because her emergency kit doesn't include the right needles … she is put on a drip, the bloke still wants us to pay, says he doesn't know anything about this insurance guarantee. Anyway you can probably guess what's coming, the idiot of a taxi driver had taken us to the wrong place. I run back to the phone to ring the insurance company who are still ringing the other hospital who are very confused about these white girls they're supposed to be treating.

It goes on, and gets worse. The hospital treats her for food poisoning even though her symptoms started before she ate anything. The ward is on the 8th floor, the lift is always full, the food is terrible and M's drip keeps emptying so her friend is terrified that air will get into her veins. But miraculously she recovers, and after a few days' bureaucracy she is released. After around 2,000 words of horror and near-death experiences, the email ends:

✉ Hope things are going okay at home. Oh yeah, I just sent 4.2 kg of saris home, guess how much it cost – £11 – and it's going to take three months to arrive!

Medical disasters can follow a gapper almost anywhere. Australia seems particularly dangerous, as this young man discovered.

✉ Right, feel free to laugh if you want (as everyone over here has). I have been in agony the last couple of days as some bloody thing decided to bite me on the ass. The bite has now become infected and hurts more than anything should. Sympathy is hard to come by when you've got such a comical injury, so laugh away if you want.

Got to go now, as I've got to meet everyone else for them to carry on laughing at my injury.

Some have much closer encounters with death, as this email from Peru reminds us. The girl and her friends go white-water rafting down a river that flows through a sacred valley.

✉ We were all kitted out in our wetsuits, waterproofs, helmets and life jackets, and had just started out on the river when our instructor started shouting instructions to us to turn the boat and back it up ... I turned around to see the body of a young woman not much older than us floating in the water face-up, our instructor asked us to grab the body and attach it to the raft, of course the 6 of us on this boat were all in shock, as it was for all of us the first dead body we had ever seen, so dumbstruck, the only thing we could do was to keep paddling. Our instructor, Eduardo, tied the body on to the boat and we had to paddle for 10 minutes till we reached a safe shore, those 10 minutes felt like an eternity, my paddle kept banging on to her body. We got her to the side and we all jumped out of the boat. No one could speak, the other 2 boats with the rest of the group hardly saw anything so were not so shaken up. We all stood in a circle and said a prayer for her.

But, of course, even a brush with the Grim Reaper will not depress our travellers for long.

✉ We carried on rafting, and luckily all was not ruined, as champagne was brought to celebrate my birthday and we stayed in a lovely campsite with an excellent view of the mountains.

Other birthdays are perhaps – with or without a corpse – not so festive. This young man celebrated his in China.

✉ First of all we found that Rhys's bank card didn't work and we had no money, but got our hotel to give us some. Then we went to a completely empty restaurant where my lavish birthday dinner cost 28 yuan (around £2) and Rhys had the shits, so didn't eat anything or drink much. Then we went to a totally empty karaoke bar, where I sang 'Happy Birthday' to myself, and went to bed by 12. Wey-hey! Anyway, could have been worse, could have had the shits myself.

Another young man came close to meeting his maker prematurely in China.

✉ We woke up to freezing weather and fucking rain. We had been preparing to do the really good mountain trail that day, so since we had nothing else to do, we climbed it anyway. The cable car was out of action, so we had to spend about 2 hours walking all the way to the top of the mountain just to reach the start of the trail. As we got higher, the weather conditions started to get really worrying, after a while we realized we were actually inside a rain cloud and our clothes were soaked through, then as we got higher the snow moved in, and an interesting survival element was added to the day. The path that we spent 2 hours climbing to get to is carved into the side of the mountain, and at times is about 4ft wide, with rock on one side, and death on the other.

When I walked this trail in the summer I remember thinking that it was a little on the dangerous side, but doing it in hard snow, with the thickest fog I've ever seen, was sick and to be honest pretty fucking pointless as the beautiful views were hidden by the bloody cloud. So it ended up being a grim 4-hour survival trek, constantly concentrating on not falling, it was so tough that at one point we were eating snow just to sustain ourselves. Anyway, what the hell, I'm still alive.

Right now I'm in Zhengzhou, the worst place in the world. It's a depressing heap of a city, imagine Milton Keynes left to rot for 100 years, and then inhabited by 8 million disgustingly ugly people who keep shouting 'HULLO! HULLO!' and muttering things under their breath about foreigners.

But relief is at hand.

✉ We couldn't get a train straight away, we had to spend the night, and this pissed us off so much that it drove us to going through with something we'd been joking about – the McHut. The McHut is very simple. First you go to McDonald's and eat loads there, and then you go to Pizza Hut and pig out on pizza. I can honestly say that I've never been so full in my life, and it had the right effect too, because for some reason Zhengzhou didn't look so bad with a bellyful of burgers and pizza.

This young woman writes from Latin America, having learned the most important lesson of all for any middle-class person from the wealthy West: however badly off you think you are, there are plenty of people worse off than yourself – infinitely worse.

✉ A very humbled Nessa is writing to you after experiencing a women's prison here in Ecuador where eight of us went to visit an English lady who is in there for drug-smuggling. We arrived and were straight away greeted with massive guns and were quite literally groped before being allowed through the gates. The smell was horrendous, the women were dressed in normal clothes, but if looks could kill none of us gringos would have come out alive. We had to bribe the head woman prisoner to let us see Terri, who is from Gloucestershire. Chatting to her was a surreal experience. She told us stories of the guards selling drugs to the prisoners, beating them to within an inch of their lives and other such pleasantries. What shocked us most was that the children of the mothers live in the prison with them, some were born in there and haven't experienced life outside ...

But once again consolation may be found around even the gloomiest corner.

☒ One of the women that we met was in there for murdering four of her children. She was a psycho and walked around with a dolly attached to her back as if it were her baby. As it was a visiting day, a lot of the prisoners had visitors, mainly old men who couldn't get action in the real world, so go there to visit the young women who are desperate for a bit of action. They bribe the guard who lets them go into a cell and do their stuff, so not only is it a prison, a drug dealers' heaven, but a brothel!

   Anyway, enough of the depressing prison chat. On a happy note I am off to the beach tomorrow to work on my tan!

Ecuadorean prisons do seem to fascinate some student travellers. This young woman also went to a prison in Quito, though one for men.

☒ Yes, it's actually true, we went to visit a couple of British prisoners doing 8 years for drug-smuggling. Jim took us around cell blocks B and C where most of the small-time dealers, thieves and murderers hang out. Fascinating, and quite amazing because they let all the prisoners out at visiting time. Mummy, I can actually hear you hyperventilating … what's really amazing is that on of the Brits admits he will continue dealing when he gets out. Apparently his friend is saving 4 kilos for him!! Everything inside the prison is so unbelievably corrupt that you can

—

actually buy your way out for $60,000 with a handshake
from the governors – good news for prisoners and innocent
backpackers alike!

Impossible to be sure, but it sounds as if this chap went to the
same prison. Possibly it features in a Rough Guide, or Lonely
Planet, or is even recommended by the local tourist board.

⊠ Went to visit a prison in Quito which was pretty scary shit,
but interesting. Was talking to one inmate in his cell (bit of
an anti-climax that I wasn't raped) and he said that you get
12 years for drug-trafficking and only 2 for murder! So if I
feel the urge to be naughty here I'm going to kill someone.
Stay well, Ollie.

The same young man rapidly gets over this experience.

⊠ In Quito, after the prison trip, I went on a crazy party bus
which was quite an experience. Everyone dances on the roof
with a band, but the bus is too tall and you have to duck for
bridges and cables. Me being too chilled out forgot to do
this. I have since been to a witch doctor, which was scary.
She was a complete nutter and made me strip so she could
beat me with flowers, and then spat all over my torso. (I was
a little freaked out by how much she knew of my fetishes.)
Penultimately I visited the Equator, which was just a line.

It is fair to say that Ecuador gets mixed reviews. This is from a
girl.

—

✉ Dear Mum and Dad and all, This place is unbelievable! We
have been here three days and it is amazing how soon you
get used to living somewhere that is at first so utterly
rancid! We now barely notice the smell of pee, the routine
of bringing water to flush down the loo without a door, the
ant armies EVERYWHERE, the gradual darkening of the pool
when the children swim, and where there were once cries
of revulsion there is now merely indulgent indifference
when Dave the (girl) puppy leaves a surprise in the middle
of our bedroom floor! However, we have been having great
fun dressing up in giant, furry animal costumes to entertain
the children …

Gappers on the whole are amazingly insouciant about their
health, at least before they get ill. This is from a young woman
in Zambia.

✉ I'm having back problems, so instead of sleeping in my bed
I have been on the concrete floor, really comfy except that
without a mozzie net I woke up covered in bites, well two
of us out of six have already had malaria, so why not make
it a third?

But when they are ill, they seem to find a certain satisfaction in
their condition. This young man emailed his parents from
Australia.

✉ I bring you now to the gruesome topic of my feet. During
my time in India, it appears that my feet had become a
touch smelly. At the time I was so into the dirty traveller

thing that I failed to notice. On arrival in Thailand, I began to notice that even touching my sandals made my hands smell, and after a great many protests from Tom and the like, I decided to get a pair of flip-flops asap. They freshened up. Throughout the rest of Thailand and Vietnam I had no problems. But on arrival in Sydney the odour, which has since become known only as 'The Rage', returned in force. Simply by leaving my shoes off, whole rooms, buildings even, would consider evacuation on account of the smell. By the end of the two weeks I had spent AU $120 on remedies and doctors. Nothing has been solved. See you all soon – I'm back in two weeks!

It'll be great to have you back in the country, son. Just don't come home!

The whole point of being on a gap year is to get things hopelessly wrong. We will all have forty-odd more years to practise getting them boringly right. This girl went to work in Ghana.

✉ Here are four more mistakes I have made since being here:
    1. Yesterday me and my friend Siobhan fell asleep on the bus and missed our stop. Had cans in hand, so obviously woke up soaking wet, in a place two hours beyond our compound.
    2. Went on a run last week, still suffering.
    3. Ate whole pot of chocolate spread yesterday.
    4. Agreed to marry this local guy, just out of sympathy, thinking would never see him again and he wouldn't recognize me – that was a big mistake, huge.

The same lass makes an even bigger mistake when she and a friend decide to visit a wildlife park in Ghana.

✉ 30 hours on a yam transportation ferry (where mice crawled all over our bodies at night), followed by several hours in a city that I would wish upon only the very worst people in the world (think Hitler, Stalin, and possibly this new boy here called Garth), then went on 2 x 7-hour bus journeys, so much sweat, so many flies due to neighbours eating fish for all seven hours and then dropping bones on my foot, then some goats and kindly chickens decided to join us. Was just about tolerating this, though the smell was so rank I thought about cutting my nose off until I thought about nose, spite, face thing and decided, although not my finest feature, I would look worse without it ... until chickens pecked my arse and I promptly burst into tears, much to everyone's amusement. Eventually arrived, and for the next five days my body was consumed with the most horrendous rash – incidentally, bird flu has reached Ghana in a big way.

To cap it all, the trip to the national park was not remotely worth the effort.

✉ After all this travelling, the baboons were 'away', the elephants were so far away that Accra, or even London Zoo was a much better option. And that's all there is. Things got worse, but I am bored of writing now, and I'm sure you're bored, so I'll stop this 'I hate Ghana' stuff. It is a shit-hole, though. I can't actually think of a worse day of my life than

that one, ever. We met some new people who arrived
today, and all were exceptionally dull / ugly / annoying. I
hate them too. I have become a really hateful person, by
the way.

Ghana is a destination that seems to bring out strong feelings.
This young woman evolved a particular loathing for one
profession there.

⊠ Taxi drivers are the bane of my life. I hate them, like REALLY
hate them. Like today for example I hailed one and after
incessant hooting, over he pulls, and when we offer our
usual price to desired destination (work … eurgh), he
laughs hysterically. Not just a snigger, but a full-on tummy-
holding, jaw-aching, banging-head-on-steering-wheel type
laughter. He then calls over a fellow cabby and tells him our
price and he too joins in the hysteria. So off we walk, and
(evidence for the success of playing hard to get) up he pulls
again, saying 'hop in'. So fine, we get in, arrive at work,
and we pay agreed price. But no, he throws a fit, and says
he thought we meant dollars. The price was 40,000 cedis,
so 40,000 dollars would probably cancel all Ghana's
national debt. So we tell him to bugger off, run into our
posh office, and he follows us. I kid you not. Chasing us. He
is now waiting outside, security wouldn't let him through,
flailing arms and all, so we can't escape for a while. Hence I
am writing a very long email to all my fellow travellers …

Visits to national parks can be a let-down. They are not all
Yosemite, or the Serengeti, or even the Peak District. This young

Canadian was in Argentina and decided to visit the park at the Peninsula Valdes. It was a seventeen-hour bus ride there, but they were promised penguins, huanacos – whatever they might prove to be – huge sealions, 'and vast expanses of bleak, bleak scrub'.

✉ The peninsula turned out to be a complete disappointment. After paying $10AR for an early bus from the nearest town, and $35 to get into the park, we discover that we cannot camp anywhere on the peninsula except on a dirt lot off the main road, because getting across the peninsula would cost $90 each for a tour, or $200 in a car, so we managed to get together an intrepid crew and each put in $30 for a local car to take us to the penguins and the sealions. I must say that the welcoming party of half a dozen dirty penguins on the other side of a fence did not exactly lift my spirits after driving for an hour along the bumpiest, dustiest road you can imagine … the highlight of our 3-hour trip may have been catching a fleeting glimpse of a tarantula at the side of the road.

This female gapper travelled all around the world. She writes in a lively and witty fashion, and is always cheerfully prepared to find the worst everywhere she goes. In Australia, because they didn't know about time differences, she and her friend missed the bus they needed to catch to reach Adelaide for her friend's plane. And her bags were already on board. So they were obliged to drive.

✉ We knew her luggage was on the bus. We knew her

passport was on there too. And we knew that she had a plane to catch in less than 24 hours in a city that was over 800 km away. Oh, sh ... The thing is, you can't really drive at night in the outback, unless you're a big fat bus, because kangaroos have a tendency to position themselves in front of small vehicles and watch them career off the road and burst into flames. So there we were, trundling along at 15 mph, leaning forward and straining our eyes to see anything that might resemble a suicidal kangaroo. After a rabbit tried its luck and scared the living bejasus out of us, we decided to call it quits and find a place to spend the night. That would be on the roadside, miles from anywhere, in the middle of a scary desert ...

They are – terrifyingly – woken by a man hammering on the side of the van. After a heart-stopping moment, it turned out to be a local inhabitant wanting to check that they were all right. And the friend made her plane.

The same student then goes to Laos.

⊠ That country was completely crackers. I thought eating river slime was a bit on the quirky side, but since then we've come across duck embryo salad, deep-fried bat and grilled squirrel. Not to mention the choice of live or dead rat at the most reputable food outlets – just so you know it's fresh.

They move on, to India.

⊠ Weighed down with bags and lack of sleep, we pick our

way through the filth-lined alleys, over piles of rotting food. Vomit lines the cobbled streets, mingling with half-eaten curries, and steaming cow poo. A passer-by spits, red liquid just missing my feet. No, this isn't Chesterfield on a Saturday night. This is Varanasi, one of the most holy cities on the Indian sub-continent. A good place to die, by all accounts. Which seems a happy coincidence, given the myriad ways you could accidentally get killed.

Her next stop is in Peru.

⊠ Never eat deep-fried guinea pig and llama kebabs before travelling on a bus for 20 hours, then boarding a light aircraft. It just doesn't work. Not unless you want to see them again, a little sooner than expected.

Some gappers, it must be said, adore the horrors they encounter and delight in passing them on. This is from a young man working temporarily as a surgeon in Australia.

⊠ The accommodation is okay, well it's interesting, a bit sticky on the floor and a few cockroaches but it's okay. I'm staying in a little place about 40 minutes from Sydney on the train, it's a small town, loads of crime, drugs etc., etc., a bit like Stoke – only less pottery though.

Life soon becomes more dramatic, even alarming. But most gap-year persons, this one included, can find the silver lining wherever it lurks.

✉ Been on and off this week, had a few quiet days, a few minor traumas. Had 2 shootings. One guy was shot in the bum and the bullet missed his major leg nerves by about 3 cm and his knackers by about 2 cm, he was a lucky chap. The other was shot 6 times – head, chest, abdomen. They opened his chest in the emergency department and he had been shot through the heart a couple of times, they tried to do all they could but there was not much hope. That was rather messy, with a nice waterfall of blood all over the floor. I'm not sure I have ever seen so much (and I have seen a lot!!!). It was not good, he was not such a lucky chap, but his knackers were intact. Helped amputate a leg with the vascular fellow, got to tie off all the vessels and suture up the muscle and skin, which was all good. I have managed to have a couple of free lunches too, which was also nice.

This is from the same temporary surgeon, who manages to find humour amid the horror. Most of us would find that tricky.

✉ The trauma was interesting and the lady was lucky to survive it. She had broken all her ribs on one side and had about 2 litres of blood in her chest with a fractured pelvis to boot, and a pre-hospital blood pressure of <60 mm HG (rule of thumb: <90 mm HG usually = very sick). She was eventually taken to theatre and they opened her chest there and she had torn one of the major vessels (azygos) in her chest, which they stitched along with a big hole in her lung. She had also torn/dissected her aorta which they fixed with a stent up from her groin and they also stopped her pelvis bleeding with a couple of coils from here too. It was pretty funny as the consultant thought he was going to have to open her tummy as it was really really swollen and he thought she may be bleeding into it big style, but she was really stable at this point, they were doing some imaging of her pelvis and noticed that she had an absolutely huge bladder and weren't sure why and they looked at her catheter and someone had clamped it shut about 10 hours previously, so they released that and her tummy went flat and saved her from another couple of hours in surgery … this weekend I am off to the Blue Mountains which are meant to be really nice. Hopefully the weather will pick up and I can enjoy some surf and a few tinnies on the beach!

The Hairy and
The Scary

In Britain we occasionally spot a squirrel, and – if you live in the
city – the foxes often come round and helpfully empty your
dustbins. But our wildlife is feeble, milk-toast stuff compared to
the beasts that live out there in gap-year land. One of the easiest
and most satisfying ways of boasting to your friends and putting
the wind up your parents is to describe your encounters – or if

you didn't actually see the fanged and venomous creatures, how you almost did. This email comes from a young woman visiting Queensland.

✉ Went naked body-surfing in the middle of the night with six boys and had to get rescued because I got dumped by an enormous wave and nearly drowned, then to add to the drama discovered that it is extremely unsafe to go swimming after dark because the sharks come inshore to feed. Not sure I'll be repeating those little escapades. Took part in a drinking competition and got fully beaten, just made it to the loos ...

A word of advice about going into the sea, anywhere abroad: don't. As this gapper in Peru discovered.

✉ Apart from all that, have been to the beach for the weekend, which was fantastic. After a 7-hour journey on a bus where we watched *Terminator II* in Spanish, we arrived and swam in the sea, had high-speed rickshaw races against each other to include high-speed rickshaw crashes, got stung by a Portuguese man-of-war while skinny-dipping in the sea at night (it might not have been a Portuguese man-of-war due to continued existence, but I didn't know that at the time, and you have never seen anyone get out of the sea quicker).

Sometimes the sea can be more welcoming than you might expect. This is from Australia.

⊠ The shark dive was quality, but we had to wait around for ages before they turned up. We waited for a couple of hours on a boat in a scene which couldn't have been more *Jaws*-like. It was a very nice day but also misty, and when we were on the boat the mist descended all around as the captain threw large bits of fish into the water. Well we waited around and eventually 2 littlish blue sharks turned up. They were about 6 and 8 feet long, but not really very vicious-looking. Then a 10/12 foot (at a guess) mako shark turned up, and though not a Great White was definitely more *Jaws*-looking, especially when the captain was pulling the fish away from it and it came out of the water. The water was freezing. The cage was bouncing around in the water and you had to be careful not to put your hand through the cage when you were holding on, it was fantastic!

All parents know that their young sons approach everything, whether bike riding or washing up, with careless nonchalance. So it must be a relief to know they are actually aware that it is inadvisable to put your fingers near to a shark's mouth.

When it comes to man-eating fish, gappers are often, to be frank, entirely bonkers. This young woman went to the Amazon.

⊠ The next morning we were awoken at 5.30 for more jungle walking, during which Victor made sure we were all acquainted with the tree whose roots look like a thousand penises, not quite touching the ground, before spying more flora and fauna from the lookout tower, and from the canoe down below it. That afternoon was spent fruitlessly piranha-fishing from the canoe, before Victor insisted that we all jump into the muddy brown water – apparently it didn't matter that we'd just been tempting man-eating fish with pieces of meat, and the water was 'perfectly safe apart from the fish that swim up your rectum …' However, having survived swimming in the Amazon, we were able to enjoy another amazing sunset fishing from the banks this time. Unfortunately we forgot a torch so Will and I were almost snapped by a caiman (3–5-metre-long member of the crocodile family) whilst trying to get back to the shore once it had got dark …

This young man and his friend go caving in China. That too may have been a mistake.

✉ I soon found myself on my belly, pushing and pulling my belly across the ground, deeper into what I thought was the final cavern, where the treasure of an underground waterfall was. Happy and exhausted, I took a picture of Hans swimming in this mini-interior waterfall, thinking the adventure was over. Never think anything. All of a sudden our guide points past, over the waterfall, and climbs up over the fall into the darkness. And so we followed, but what became quickly apparent was we were not alone. I am not talking about the fish beneath our feet, or the worms in the rocks, I am talking about bats. Hans had rushed ahead, we quickly shouted 'Wow, bats!' As soon as he said this, the bats shot past the corner into our faces. What followed was bats swarming around our heads trying to keep out of the torch's light. It did cross my mind in a panic, shit, should have had that rabies jab, but after a while I became accustomed to the nippy flying rodents. Anyway, I didn't get bitten, so I won't be in search of virgin's blood or foaming at the mouth, biting my own hand.

Africa, of course, has quite a selection of unwanted beasts:

⊠ After I left the internet place we went to do a shop in the supermarket and we walked in to find that a man was putting up a sign (well, that's what we thought). He was actually holding down a rat with the sign and another guy was hitting it with a broom to try and kill it, lovely!!!! ... had a freak-out on Wednesday as saw a tarantula in the house, huge bloody thing so hairy and gross, so typically it would be a day for creepy-crawlies, 2 more spiders on the walls, and then centipede things!!!

This is from Panama.

⊠ I meticulously arrange my mozzie net in the mornings and evenings, wrapping it across and under the sponge mattress, so you can imagine my horrific surprise to discover a very dangerous scorpion hanging from the roof of the net. I called him Paul Daniels, and he met with the sharp side of a colleague's machete. Would have been a trip to hospital.

Mind you, some people visiting Africa hope and expect to encounter wildlife. This young man is spending time in Kenya.

✉ We have been doing a lot of camping and I am getting pretty expert. We go to one of the bomas and set up camp inside their walls to protect us from wild beasts and such (a boma is a small collection of huts). Sometimes it is so difficult – we arrive at the poorer bomas and are surrounded by snotty kids covered in flies, they think they are lucky because they are associated with livestock, their favourite things, and don't understand all our stuff about 'they carry diseases', and emaciated dogs all covered in sores, and you just know that the ground is covered in animal and small child waste (no Pampers here) and human spit, and I don't want to touch anything, but mostly it's great …

We have had lots of exciting snake incidents. Went with Julian to a nearby airfield to drop some bracelets and on the way back we saw a huge spitting cobra, it was crossing the road in front of us, we both saw it, leaned forward for a better look, realized what it was, leaned back, checked our sunglasses were on firmly, but luckily it shot off and didn't spit! Also moved my bag on Monday and found a snake under it, just a baby, but it lunged at me, and I got someone to get rid of it (they claimed it was a black mamba, but as the Masai hate snakes and claim every one is a deadly killer, you have to take that with a pinch of salt!).

The other really exciting animal encounter was, I saw my first leopard! We were driving back from dropping off another volunteer at the airfield, and went along a river because they knew I really wanted to see a leopard and there are lots of trees there and it's the most likely spot, and we looked and looked until I fell asleep, and Jenny suddenly grabbed me and I woke up to see a leopard crossing in front of us. We interrupted it hunting, so it then went and sulked under a tree and we got a really good look.

Snakes? You haven't seen snakes if you haven't been to South America. This young woman was on safari in Venezuela.

✉ I should mention that during one of our safaris I nearly needed a change of underwear when we stumbled across a 3.5 metre ana-fucking-conda. Are you understanding that? 3.5 metres. Our guide, a local called Papas, who in my opinion should have his own show, casually poked it with a stick and did some 'I am clearly not 100% sane' moves to catch it. Then he offered us 'goes' at holding it. It took about 5 adults to hold it, and I have photos to prove my claims.

Things are not helped when your travelling companions are in league with the more alarming fauna. This is from a young Scottish woman in Burma. She, like many gappers, seems to be under the impression that an exclamation mark is a useful vowel.

✉ We're in a place called Batu Patay (or however it's spelled) which is a tiny village next to a big river. In hammocks under tarps, there are bugs everywhere! And they're huge!!!!! But am having a really good time. All the people are wicked! And there is a store in the village and a volleyball court, so fun messing around with locals. Guy beside me just farted. Eeeewww!!!! Anyway, I've seen a ton of monkeys and I saw a croc the other day!!! Bit disconcerting as they live in the river that we are beside!!!!! Today we visited an orang-utan sanctuary which made me think of Becky!!!! Just joking!!! Saw lots of freaky monkeys too!!!!

The same lass goes for a walk through the jungle.

⊠ Just been trekking for 12 days, but group underestimated food rations rather badly as we couldn't be bothered to carry them, so pretty much was starving after 12 days of plain porridge and plain crackers and plain rice for dinner, eeewww, anyhow last night we went out for dinner and three of us ate so much they threw up, and no one could move after dinner, very amusing!!! Now off to go diving for a week on desert island!!! Wahooooooo, where there is café so no more shit shit shit food!!! Mozzies not so bad trekking, but fuck me there are some big ass bugs here. Got one crazy Malaysian guy in my group who finds it really funny to chase me with the bugs he catches!

It is quite awe-inspiring to learn how brave some of our gappers are. They march into jungles with the same casual ease with which at home they might enter a branch of Top Shop. This email is from Ecuador, which may offer more strange experiences per square mile than any other gap-year destination.

⊠ Spiders the size of your hand, cockroaches, weird insects, mice, crocodiles, pink dolphins (yes, that's right!), monkeys, racoons, butterflies, sloths, anacondas, parrots, macaws, piranhas … all these things were in the jungle and so were we! Didn't see everything, we were very gutted that we didn't see any jaguars, but maybe that's a good thing. Also didn't see the crocs, but we did see the anaconda, and yes it was scary, but not all that big, maybe three metres, but it was all curled up. I think it looked kind of cute!

We stayed in a kind of tree-house in the middle of the jungle. It was an eco-tour thingy, so everything was pretty basic, but I'm used to that now!!! It was facing the jungle and if there was anything out there I would have got a good view!!! It was kind of scary, though, I'll admit. I wouldn't want to be left there on my own. It is so noisy at night time … I forgot my earplugs and I could hear growling (which was the howler monkeys – apparently) and munching and scampering in our room. God knows what that was. The scariest thing we did was a night canoe trip, searching for caimans, the crocodiles they have there. I wasn't really too keen on the idea of being in a very small boat in the dark, when if you go in the water you probably won't come out again!!! We didn't get to see any crocs because we ran out of fuel … that was a bit scratchy as it was very dark and very quiet and we were in the middle of the Amazon river.

Others are less lucky. This is from West Africa.

✉ On Wednesday we went up to Wa in order to go to the hippo sanctuary, but as you do here, we ended up waiting five and a half hours in what the guidebook calls 'the most fascinating town'. Er … I think he should get a life. We didn't get to Wechiau, the village near the hippos, until after dark. Early morning sanctuary visit was as predicted. We saw lots of hippos. Albeit all were under water, but the ears are the best bit, I swear. So don't trust these guidebook people who send you off on detours to crap places where there is nothing to do.

Here is another – possibly apocryphal – example of human beings teaming up with animals to scare innocent gap-year students.

☒ The Chinese have a very wicked trick that they play on foreigners and even though every foreigner is told about the story they fall for it their first time, every time. I have been told the story, and apparently it is only a matter of time before I am lured into it. What happens is this: the Chinese have a method of frying a fish so that it is still alive, even though it looks dead on the plate. There is one particular dish in which the fish is covered in breadcrumbs but remains alive. Apparently when the dish is served discreetly to a foreigner, the foreigner jabs it with his chopsticks and the fish jumps two feet high off the plate!!!

Not all animals are dangerous, although they do seem to be malevolent. This is from a volunteer working in Peru.

☒ The food is weird, the water is brown, and there are more bugs than plants (and that's saying something). The rats scuttle around the rooms at night and eat any food left out. It is SO hot, more hot than you would ever think, and humid and sweaty and gross. I have my own little room

which I lock to keep out the monkeys, who got into another
girl's room and broke her iPod and stole her malaria tablets.
But it's not as bad as it sounds!

A week later she is bringing her mother up to date.

⊠ My tummy is a little rumbly but completely controllable
and I think it will be better in a few days' time. I just have
to finish adjusting to the water. Have you sent my bras yet?
The monkeys have gone a step further. They wait until
we're all doing stuff and break the electricity to our rooms,
so night comes and our lights won't go on. It's easily fixable
but on a nightly basis it is rather trying! We are working on
a plan to watch the main evil monkey and strand him on an
island further upstream so he can't come back ...

The most surprising animals can turn out to be dangerous –
especially in Australia.

⊠ We headed for Byron Bay, only a 2–3-hour drive apparently,
it took us about 7. So we stopped in Coffs Harbour for a
night as we were all tired and emotional, and Ivan the
driver was starting to complain. So we stayed in a tiny
campsite and I saw an animal [I didn't recognize]. It was
quite funny really because it jumped into a palm tree we
were passing on the way to the bathroom, it gave us a bit
of a shock and we weren't sure what it was, so we looked
up into the tree. Being the tallest, I reckoned I knew pretty
well what it was. 'It's okay, it's only a cat ... with short arms.
Yeah, a cat with short arms, no problem.' Terri looked at me

quizzically. 'A what?!' I looked confused, looked at her, and looked at an amused bystanding man. 'What's a cat with short arms in this country, then?' I asked him. 'That? Oh, that's a possum. Don't look so frightened. They haven't killed anyone for at least 2 or 3 years.' I had to sit in the bathroom for 20 minutes until I was sure it had gone.

Better to Travel
Hopefully

You see your child off at the airport, with a niggling voice at the back of your head asking insistently whether this might be the last time you set eyes on them. But at least they are going to spend the next few hours in the relative comfort of an aeroplane. Cramped it may be, and the food indifferent, but compared to what they are about to face it might as well be an upper-deck stateroom on the old *Queen Elizabeth*. There are no carry-on chickens or dead fish on the row in front. You will not have to share your seat with another passenger. The chances of bandits holding up the plane and robbing everyone on board are minimal. However, a terrible reality waits for them at the other end.

The most common form of transport for gappers visiting the Third World is, of course, the bus. These are rarely luxury coaches with TVs and toilets, nor do they even offer the comforts of the number 12 bendy bus to Peckham. But, as in this email from India, they can be a lot more exciting.

✉ A four-hour drive from Jabalpur, in turn a 17-hour train journey from Delhi, the drive across mud tracks, women carrying massive baskets on their heads etc. It was a hectic drive, visibility was 5 metres and the giant trucks do not use lights going at 50 mph, we saw two crashes, and then our driver hit some man at 30 mph, full on, seriously scary, the windscreen was smashed but the driver just drove on. It is so backward here!!!! Luckily he 'only' fractured his leg and his head was bleeding, not great when the hospital is a mud hut. On more lovely things, neither of us have had the Delhi belly despite the most ludicrously spicy chicken/rat curry on the train and other delights.

Nor do schedules count for very much. This is from Laos.

✉ Pretty much everything here is made of bamboo or teak, with the exception of the roads which are generally made of much less durable substances, like mud. Nothing happens quickly here, and so transport timetables do not exist. Invariably one goes to the sort of 'bus' station where you wait until there are enough people going somewhere to fill up the truck. This may take hours. It is necessary that the back of the truck is implausibly overcrowded before departure, thus creating a suitably Communist sense of camaraderie and mutual discomfort.

Our ride today provided extra amusement when two ladies climbed on with a veritable menagerie of beasts. Besides the unremarkable selection of chickens and ducks they also had a couple of beaver-like animals that may or may not be called 'bamboo rats'. One was alive-ish but looking a bit off colour, the other unarguably dead. One of them pulled out a squirrel from a bag, and it was here that the dramatic tension lay, for the squirrel was in an ambiguous state. Occasionally the lady would hold her squirrel out of the window for a while to afford it a little air, and this she would follow with a little gentle heart massage. At this point the little fella would open his eyes and waggle his feet before lapsing back into a coma again. The woman then looked over at me with a knowing shake of the head which said 'I did my best, but death comes to us all', and bunged the squirrel back in the basket, sealing its fate by plonking a large dead bamboo rat on top. Thus enlightened, we continued to Luang Prabang where we are now.

You can learn much about a country from its bus services. This is from central Africa. Like some gap-year emails it is cunningly designed first to worry the receiving 'rents and then reassure them.

✉ It did take us 6 hours to get there, and we didn't hitch-hike, daddy, we used the minibuses!! Bloody nightmare, though, it takes forever to get anywhere in this country!! Had some interesting experiences on the way. In our bus there were about 50 people (and we're not talking a big bus either) and then a guy at the side of the road flagged down the bus and was holding a 3-foot catfish, dead but absolutely stank!! Oh yes, he decided to get on so we all had the company of a bloody huge fish for about an hour. These journeys just seem to get better and better!!!!

Anxious parent thinks, 'Oh, so that's all right, if a smelly fish is the worst she has to put up with ...'

This is from Honduras.

✉ Well, the other day we left Utila. Travelled all day to the capital of Honduras, which was actually way better than everyone made it out to be (as in, you walk down the streets and get SHOT). So yesterday we left for the journey from hell. First a lovely three and a half hour journey with very uncomfy seats and music so loud you could hardly hear yourself think. Then a minibus to the Nicaraguan border. We got out of the bus to be surrounded by men trying to get you into their little bicycle cab thingy, poking you, shouting. However, their work was in vain seeing as the guy couldn't open the boot to get our bags out. We waited for almost an hour in the blazing heat while tons of men tried desperately to open the boot. They finally concluded it was hopeless so they loaded the bus with people and us, ready to take us back to where we had come from (a tiny little scummy town where I would rather eat a tampon than sleep).

Thankfully they got the boot open and a collective cheer rang out as the men all grabbed our bags and us, and forced us into their bike/cab thingies. We got through the border and they charged us $20 each!!!! Which is more than we've paid for anything! Emily was ready to kill someone, but seeing as we were surrounded by angry men, one of whom came up really close to me and licked his lips, I was like 'Emily, pay and go NOW!' so we got on a bus full of local women, ready for the 3 and a half hour journey to Leon.

Latin America is never easy.

⊠ The first time we tried to get into Paraguay we got deported over a dispute over entry tax. This immigration official got on the bus and hauled us off, then tried to make us pay some mystery tax which we were having none of. He took us into the room with loads of armed guards, and tried to intimidate us into giving him the money. To cut a long story short, we ended up getting escorted to the border. But it was all right, we went in the back way next day.

Or take this scary adventure in Mexico.

⊠ Anyhow, yesterday was meant for going to Oaxaca, however had a slight mishap along the way, as there was a teachers' strike and we got a few hours outside to find the road blocked, and the teachers had set fire to a bus and

were carrying rocks and bats, and we heard gun shots, at
this point, 3 a.m., all we wanted to do was go back, but
half the bus didn't want to, so we sat there for another hour
or so until the bus driver made the decision to go all the
way back, 6 hours, what a nightmare.

Having an amazing time, can't believe I have only a
month left, and then it's all over!!!!

And our government complains about the 'militant' teachers of
the NUT. When did you last see petrol bombs stored in the staff
room?

It's a common experience for gappers to find that just when
they think everything has been sorted out, it suddenly gets much
worse. Or the police arrive. Or both. The email continues:

✉ We'd been driving for 15 minutes when the bus was
stopped and was searched by the police, the women
frantically started packing things away under their skirts and
tried to get us to take their packages!!!!!! So the bus turned
around and headed back to the border, 20 minutes at the
border and we set off again, only to be stopped AGAIN by
the police. But they let us go, and the driver drove so, so
fast for a bit. Didn't really know if we were being chased or
not! So we got to Leon ... woke up at 6 this morning to
what I'm sure was gunfire. We are in an open dorm and I
have NEVER been that scared in my life. At one point it
sounded like someone was shooting at the hostel door. My
heart was pounding, I was shaking, could hardly breathe
and felt sick. In fact I don't want to talk about it cos it
makes me feel all those things again even tho' it's light out!

—

This young man took a very long journey from Brazil, into Argentina, and learned that buses can bring other perils.

✉ Just spent 36 hours on a bus with a Brazilian who thought he could speak English but it sounded more like Elfish. He was wearing a lime green shirt, and kept on asking me GCSE French oral-style questions about siblings, likes and dislikes, etc. to practise. After five hours I got bored, and made up many contrasting personas. I now have three black, orange-haired cousins who live in Sweden. But I don't, so got bored talking about them after a while. I got so desperate, I made myself sick on him. (Didn't really, I just swallowed all manners and found the only other seat available on the bus, next to the non-flushing loo, but I figured my sense of smell was a fair trade.)

But gappers love to find fun and excitement amid the worst privations. This is from South America.

✉ Hey guys, tips to entertain you on your next sleepless bus journey.
   1. Game called 'List it'. Write down the letters of the alphabet and try to think of definitive brand names for every one. It's a hoot.
   2. Articulate … make up your own. It's amazing.
   3. Teach fellow foreign travellers English songs, but to different tunes. That's a challenge. Although, 'If you wanna be my lover' to the tune of '*Jerusalem*' is not the ideal soundtrack for 17 hours on a bus.
   4. Other greats include: charades, sticker on forehead

game, although when playing with aforementioned
Germans avoid the classic dictator. (We thought they were
Dutch.)

Northern China appears to have a service which even our own
shambolic privatised bus companies would blench at. This
comes from a particularly adventurous young woman travelling
with a friend.

✉ We arrived at the Altai bus station in Urumqui and booked
a ticket to Buerjin (Burqin) in northern Xinjiang, a rather
remote destination, but we were encouraged by the fact
that there were no other Westerners in the bus station, only
Uighurs selling baked whole goats, with a fetching red
ribbon around their spiced skulls, always a good omen in
my books. So we bought a ticket and eventually managed
to locate our bus (the old rickety type that has transported
too many live pigs in its day). Of course we soon found out
why our tickets were slightly less expensive than we had
expected, turns out we had the back bunk at the top, and
we had to share it with four other people, which is no mean
feat. If you're a typical bony, verging on slightly emaciated-
looking Chinese, then this poses no problem, but two
healthy foreigners is a different story altogether, lots of
kicking, elbowing, foot shuffling had to ensue before we
successfully managed to install ourselves in a seat and stake
enough territory to at least have minor leg-manoeuvring
capabilities. It appeared that we were going to have to
share the back seat with four other people, a rather
corpulent Muslim, a shrivelled old Chinese woman, a man

clad in army surplus gear, a young boy in a Juventus T-shirt, and a cat, so it appeared we'd drawn the short straw. About 2 km out of town it became apparent that we weren't so much on a road as on a dirt track, which appeared to have been built in a pre-industrialized era, before the advent of well, anything that you would associate with road-building. What then ensued was 16 hours of non-stop head bashing, gripping on to a window, or bag, or fellow passenger, anything to prevent that fatal collision with the ceiling. I think the cat was grabbed at one stage, much to its personal dismay. It got so bad that at one stage Imogen's head actually punctured the ceiling and nearly made contact with the metal shell of the bus, much to the amusement of our fellow passengers. (Loud chortling was also heard from the direction of the bus driver, think he was aiming for those potholes on purpose.) Eventually Imogen decided that the floor of the bus looked like a more comfortable option. It has its benefits – you have to go further before hitting the roof, though you do get trampled on those sporadic, middle of the night, middle of nowhere, stops for the toilet.

Nothing stops our gappers, least of all a Chinese cat and a hole in the bus's roof. Undeterred, the two girls continue heading north towards Kazakhstan.

✉ On sighting an unidentifiable alien, people swarm round you like a pack of famished vultures. We were being quoted 800 yuan, 200 yuan, $150, nobody would tell us how much it should really cost for the 5 to 6 hour journey there and we were told that we could not pay for a single, one-way trip, but a return, where we would have to arrange the pick-up date, sounded highly dubious to us, and it's not exactly the first thing you want to deal with while nursing a bus-invoked headache. So we decided to get away from the mob and grab some lunch, more mutton and yak tea for us, mmmmm, appetizing. We had been back at the bus station for about an hour when we were approached by a young Kazakh boy, who said that he was going to Hanas in a truck and they needed two more people to fill the seats and split the price. It would be 75 yuan for the one-way trip. It sounded good to us, so we climbed aboard, first stop, the garage, where there were a few 'minor problems' with the engine, oh well, nothing serious there then, yes I know, a bell or two should have been ringing at that stage. Anyway, after three hours, stuck in a grimy coalyard, we eventually got back on the road.

You will be unsurprised to learn that, while the scenery is sensational, the truck is not quite up to the job of passing through it.

✉ Halfway up a particularly nasty hill, the engine gave out and we found ourselves in the rather unexpected position of rolling back down the hill. We jumped out and much shouting and swearing in Kazakh ensued, before the father of the family was eventually instructed by the driver to quickly throw a large stone or boulder under the back tyre. It was a weird spectacle, and reminded me somewhat of the hammer-throwing in the Olympics. He managed to hoist a

stone on to his shoulder and throw it in the general
direction of the car, luckily it managed to lodge behind the
back wheel, to rounds of applause from the rest of us. The
driver attempted to restart the engine to no avail. So we
waited by the side of the road, as dusk finally settled,
waiting for a truck coming our way that might give us a
tow to the top. We scanned the horizon for the distant
rumble of wheels on stone, or the resultant cloud of dust,
all eyes were focused on the road. After about 40 minutes
our ears pricked up as we heard a low murmur and a hazy
shroud of desert sand rose in the air, our hearts began to
beat faster, it was growing cold and there was no protection
out here, all hopes were pinned on this oncoming vehicle,
we were going to be rescued at last. It was at that point
that the herd of yaks rounded the corner ...

But the truck is coaxed into life, and somehow they manage the
five-hour journey in only twelve hours, spending a wonderful
three days in Hanas (Kanas), which is on the border of four
countries – China, Russia, Mongolia and Kazakhstan.

They seem to have been lucky, however, compared to these
young women, who decide to take the bus over the Himalayas
to Leh, in Kashmir, in the far north of India. This carries them,
or tries to carry them, over passes up to 15,000 feet high. They
start in the town of Manali, where it is pouring with rain.

⊠ Eventually the bus turns up, no room in the boot for our
bags so they're chucked on the roof. 'Yes, yes, madam,
waterproof, 10 rupees please.' And the journey begins.

Except that it's still pissing down and the spectacular view is slightly blocked by massive clouds and it's bloody terrifying swerving around the tight corners, literally a single-lane road with a complete cliff drop over the edge, screeching to a halt now and again to let a lorry pass, praying it stays that inch away from us and doesn't knock us over the edge … now we've reached the first of four passes, this one going up to over 4,000 metres above sea level (that's high to me and you). The rain (that still hasn't stopped) turns to snow, a blizzard in fact. Glaciers thicker than the height of the bus have been chopped in half to make way for the road, we pass trucks abandoned in thick snow, it turns out our windscreen wipers don't really work, and I've never felt so cold in my life, 4 jumpers, 2 blankets, 2 pairs of socks, a hat and gloves, and we're still shivering.

Eventually, against all the odds, we reach the end of the pass, a little village in a valley with a police checkpoint and chai stalls. No toilets, though, so we have to run up the hill in the pouring rain. A half-hour stop turns into a 4-hour stop and eventually we find out that we can't go on because the Leh road has been destroyed by landslides and heavy rain. It's too dangerous for us to go back to Manali through the blizzard (which we had just come through, wish someone had told us that) so we settle down for long, comfortable (!?) night on the bus … we're parked down the road from the shops so every time we want food or chai we have to make a 200-metre dash in the heavy rain. We don't want to get all our clothes wet, they take too long to dry, so before we get off the bus I take off my blankets, skirt and socks, roll up my trousers to my knees, put on my flip-flops,

yes, that is as painful as it sounds, but worth it to get back
into everything when you're back on the bus. Glad I
brought my -3 degrees sleeping bag, some people didn't.

It gets worse. They're told they will have to stay a few days until
it stops raining, when it will be possible to repair the road. Thirty
or forty travellers are crammed into the lobby of a guesthouse,
where they can sleep on the concrete floor. They retrieve their
luggage from the roof rack, and find it all completely soaked.
Finally the sun comes out, and the buses head back for Manali,
pausing only to crash into a jeep on the way.

Things are little better in Kenya.

⊠ According to Rough Guide, Mount Elgon should only be
attempted by four-wheel drive, but this was obviously a
typo because the bus made a valiant attempt, though when
we got out at the park gates the water tank exploded and
blew the front seat out, which we probably should have
taken as a warning sign. Unperturbed, about 15 boys and
the three of us sat on the roof to see the buffalo and the
bus set off up the mountain. It didn't get very far before the
engine cut out, we started rolling backwards down a steep
slope, all the girls were screaming, Trish had hold of me by
the back of my T-shirt, so I didn't slide down the side of the
bus, and one boy got so worried he jumped off. We were
saved by a large rock which the rear wheel hit, tearing a
hole in the bottom.

Think that's bad? Try Vietnam, from which a young female

gapper wrote an email headed 'My Private Hell'. She takes a van to cross from Laos into Vietnam. This proves to be a mistake.

✉ I have been scared of heights all my life. So imagine my delight, as we came over the brow of the hill, just over the border, to see not merely sheer vertical drops falling away from us into mist-covered oblivion, not just a winding mountain pass consisting entirely of hairpin bends snaking blindly into thick fog, but no barrier, no markings, no edge to the road. But thick slippery mud, more than a foot deep, and piles of rock and rubble, fallen from the cliff sides above, all covering the road, if you can call it a road. And the moisture from the freezing fog had turned its surface into slippery, trickling slop, that fell away from the cliff edge into nothingness. Did I mention I was scared of heights?

I wanted to get out and walk, but I didn't trust my shaking legs to carry me. We slipped and our wheels skidded not inches from the edge. On two occasions the van door swung open and the fella wedged next to me nearly fell out. In the true spirit of pathetic fallacy the weather turned grey and sinister, and we were met by a procession of miserable images, including a lorry stacked high with boxes of half-dead dogs, headed for the wok.

The same student goes to Thailand, and makes another mistake – she gets on a bus there too.

✉ In an attempt to beat karma at its own game, when we got to Bangkok we bought a deep-fried scorpion, thinking 'you bite us, we'll eat you'. Problem was, it tasted repulsive, and we had to wash it down with a bag of deep-fried crickets. And I think it pissed off someone up there, one of those many-armed dog / monkey / pigeon / gods with an interest in maintaining balance in these parts. Although causing our bus to career off the motorway and into three cars seemed a little unfair. It's okay, no one was hurt. I just remember Daisy calmly looking up from a back-seat game of cards and saying slowly, 'We're all going to die.'

How very different from the bus ride in, say, Birmingham, where students catch the 11.30 a.m. early-morning service to Edgbaston. Other people make a different mistake – they decide to transport themselves independently, like this young man in Thailand.

✉ I was briskly taken through the workings of a motorbike, a large, throbbing motorbike. It all seemed fairly basic, so I flung myself astride this thing, enthusiastic, anticipating exploration of the island. I pootled for about 5 metres where I had to get off again for George to get gas. Then it all went pear-shaped. Started the engine, teased the throttle, and the bloody thing ran off. *You've Been Framed* would have had a field day as my motor careered away from me, then collapsed head first into another rank of hire bikes. Five minutes later, looking bemused, I was surrounded by hordes of Thais, all claiming links with one or other of the damaged bikes. My wallet has been relieved of £150.

River travel can be just as perilous.
✉ Unbelievably, neither me nor Vanessa has experienced any

kind of bottom problem since being away (famous last words!). In fact, the lack of toilets was the least of our problems on the slow boat down the Mekong. Try 8 hours on a wooden plank with no room to stand, nowhere to put your feet, and a freezing cold wind blowing through your now-soaked clothes, thanks to that really big wave at the start. But to be fair, our Mekong experience was a true pain / pleasure combo. The first day was, I'll admit, an exercise in endurance, but after that our luck changed. We found a guesthouse that boasted 'Electric Light Bulb' (not to be sneezed at in these parts) and next day we boarded a boat that had just that extra foot of head room, just those 2 extra inches for your feet, that made everything bearable. Granted, the extra room was for cargo, and soon enough we were loading up with rice sacks, coconuts, random hitch-hikers, some chickens, and a pig. (The pig was wrapped entirely in wicker, so that it looked just like a wicker pig, but we knew it was a real pig because it kept squealing, particularly when one of the crew members accidentally dropped it in the river. It's okay, they fished it out again.) I soon discovered that a sack of rice, no matter how tightly packed, is infinitely more easy on the arse than a wooden plank. And besides, it was a sunny day and the scenery just spectacular. Worth a numb bum.

These young women were travelling around Kenya.

✉ After leaving the Masai Mara we travelled north to a campsite by a hippo-infested lake. Buses seem to be the best way to get about here but the drivers are maniacs! It seems they prefer to drive in the ditches in order to preserve the tarmac on the roads. Crazy, and they stuff as many people on as well so the whole experience is a B.O. nightmare … none of the distances on the map seem to be accurate, which resulted on Sunday in a 25-mile bike ride to a lake. This was a seriously SH 1 T day. As previously explained, road conditions are not excellent. Nearly fell into a ditch due to crap brakes, and much of the journey was spent walking as the roads turned into sandy tracks. At one point I was struggling up a hill and a herd of about 100 cattle came hurtling down the hillside towards me. Being bicycly-challenged I ditched my bike in the road and ran away. On the way back we also managed to trespass on some colonial's land by accident and were chased by 6 snarling and barking dogs. Yesterday was also hardcore, as we walked around a national park, which ended up being a 3-mile hike, again due to awful signs everywhere. Stopped for lunch for a rest but after about 2 minutes a baboon jumped on to our picnic table and snatched our bread away! Thankfully Tom won the battle and the bread was not lost.

The thing that gnaws away at most parents is the knowledge that their gap-year students are not always, perhaps, quite as alert as they should be. Even at home, they tend to miss the last bus then realize they have no money for a taxi back. Or they forget to set the alarm the night before a crucial interview. How much worse it must be, we fear, when they are in a foreign land without us to rescue them from their own muddle-headedness. This is from a young woman visiting South Africa with friends.

✉ Cape Town is amazing. Had an incredibly exciting (in hindsight) night yesterday. Picture this: we're walking out of a club at about 3 a.m. All slightly the worse for wear (i.e. all had been violently sick, spent much of the evening table-dancing, and think I swapped my, albeit rank, watch for a plastic cowboy hat). Get into nearest taxi. Ed passes over a card with the address of our hostel on, and taxi heads up the hills. Five minutes later we are all fast asleep. Two hours later, we are still asleep and still in the taxi and it is still moving. Finally, 5.20 a.m., and it suddenly dawns on me that we are in a strange place, the meter is something ridiculous like 1,000 rand (about £100) and the driver is still driving, so I start screaming abuse at Mr Taximan. Images from *The Bone Collector* induce further panic and more yelling. Ed and Soph drunkenly awaken and become equally psychotic. The Taximan eventually pulls up, flashes us a beaming, yet confused smile to reveal an array of gold teeth and only one eye – not perfect for a taxi driver. We frantically try to open the doors, but is it really a good idea to be stranded on an abandoned road on the outskirts of one of the most dangerous cities in the world? He leaned back and pointed at the card we had given him. Upon further inspection, still petrified of our one-eyed, golden-toothed, murderer / kidnapper / rapist / thief taxi-driver, we realized that Ed had handed over the card of our next hostel – only 200 miles down the coast.

But even airports have their hazards, as this young man discovered.

✉ Well guys, I'm stuck at bloody Bangkok airport waiting for a flight that leaves in 9 hours. No one speaks English, have just been sick three times courtesy of breakfast, and I'm being stalked by a very weird woman with one arm, and one leg (yup, so I am able to run away). In addition to this I spent the whole of last night and day before in Bombay airport, I have had an hour's sleep in the last 48, and I want my mummy.

As Paul Theroux will tell you, trains can provide some of the most exciting of all travel adventures. This is from a young woman who's been travelling south through Russia, trying to reach Mongolia.

✉ Dear Mum, well, I hardly know where to begin this time. I'm in Ulan Bator now after a bit of a fiasco. We had left Irkutsk and bought ticket to Mongolia, we had been on the train for a day already and we pulled into Naushki, a small town that's on the border with Mongolia, we were told that the train would stop there for at least two hours, which turned out to be more like five hours, we were waiting in the heat because everyone had to get off the train as only two of the ten carriages would proceed to Mongolia, after about four hours the border officials arrived, after taking the usual Russian attitude of prolonging affairs for as long as possible ... so we finally re-boarded the train and handed over our visas and passports. Another hour passed, as we waited in the sweltering heat, we were asked to fill out declaration forms, the usual sort, 'are you carrying any nuclear materials, do you have any illegal Russian orphans smuggled in your baggage?' type thing, there was also a

section where you had to declare any valuables and notes in
foreign currency or travellers' cheques. So I wrote down
$250 and thought nothing of it. Five minutes before we
have to leave, they come back and say there is a 'big
problem', two words we had heard before in Belarus and
which did not sound very promising …

It is the start of a horrible nightmare. The officials won't let her
return to the train without changing her money into Russian
roubles, even though she is leaving Russia and the bank in the
station is closed. A crooked money-lender offers her a ridiculous
exchange rate which, in desperation, she accepts. Meanwhile her
friend is still on the train. Horribly, unbelievably, this now starts
to pull away.

✉ The train has gone, and so has the dodgy money-lender
with my money. My head was completely scrambled, I'm
just in a state of shock that the train has gone, I wander
back into the station waiting hall and realize that Sally has
all our Russian money, all our food, and half my possessions.
The Russian official with incredibly cold eyes comes back
and hands me back my passport with a stamp over my visa
which says that I have been unable to cross the border. I try to
plead and tell him I don't even have a ticket to Ulan Bator
because the carriage attendant never gave it back, he just
stares at me blankly and walks off with a smirk on his face.

At least she is not alone. Four Czech travellers are in the same
situation. They all decide to get away from the corrupt officials
(who know how much money they have on them). That night

they stay in a boarding house, and figure the best plan is to get a car to the border the next day. The plan seems to be working, but next morning their driver is stopped by the police who tell him he can't go any further. Luckily a bus turns up, they reach the border crossing and by the kind of miracle that occasionally happens to gap-year students, another bus, full of Korean tourists and with a few spare seats, lets them on to travel free. But they do have to get past a new set of officials.

⊠ This time it was two friendly peroxide women. I lied and said I had no currency, which they accepted quite gladly. Now it was my turn to confront the guard, the passport control guy. I presented my passport, with my horrible stamped visa. I smiled politely and tried to look composed, he took absolutely ages, staring at my passport, staring at me, typing things into the computer, re-typing them, so there I was, growing increasingly nervous, longing to hear that noise when the stamp finally goes on the visa – talk about a test of nerves. Finally he felt he had tortured me long enough and I was able to pass through into Mongolia, the promised land! The relief of climbing on to that bus was indescribable ... the journey through that vast deserted land was quite surreal, as the Koreans had purchased a bottle of cheap Russian vodka and got very tipsy – picture rolling plains and a vast blue sky, while beside you two middle-aged Korean men are Hawaiian-dancing up the aisle while singing 'Auld Lang Syne' in their best Scottish accents ...

Could you tell me what marks I got in my individual units, because in London I could only discover whether I had passed or not?

—

Finally she reaches Ulan Bator, and is reunited with her friend.

This young woman has been spending a year in northern Russia which included the appallingly cold winter of 2005–6.

✉ The trip to Moscow for my parcel turned out really well, though at first it seems like a real chore because I had to get there and back on the Sunday, which meant 11 hours on the train. In the end my friends Lo and Tasha came with me, and because everything was closed on Sunday, we abandoned our vague plans to do with culture, and ended up consuming 3 times our combined body weight in steak and wine. This was fine until we decided it was time to head back to Yaroslav and by mistake got on the train to Chita – a small town 8 time zones away, on the border with China. Luckily we realised our mistake in time to get off at the next stop, but if we hadn't the train wasn't going to stop for another four days and this email would have been from Siberia.

Anyway, we finally got on the right train, but ended up sharing a carriage full of drunk 'businessmen'. One of them had passed out in the loo, so to punish him the scary, scary conductor-woman had locked him in for the duration of the journey. Unfortunately this meant that we had to pee in between the carriages on to the tracks while the train was still moving. This required us to be agile, firm-footed and resistant to the outside temperature (minus 25). I was none of the above, but my pea-sized bladder forced me to try my luck. Sadly the train lurched while I was pulling up my trousers, and my bottom froze to the metal outside of the train. I have never been in such a quandary. The idea of tearing myself off and leaving the best part of my bottom stuck to the Yaroslav express was horrifying, but the alternative, staying there until spring, was equally unattractive. Eventually I wrenched myself free, but I fear my poor buttocks will never be the same again.

Because of all the drunken shenanigans around us, we decided to lie low in our compartment, nursing my bottom and a bottle of vodka. The man sharing our compartment was the only one not part of the group of plastered mafiosi. Unluckily for him, the other men discovered that there were English girls in the neighbouring compartment and tried to come in. Sergei (the nice man) tried feebly to stop them coming in and started arguing with them in Russian. They told him to come out and have a cigarette with them, and he went, albeit v. reluctantly. A few minutes later, they all came back and sat down with us. Sergei had a black eye and a cut lip. He didn't complain any more on our behalf, thank goodness.

'Rent Control

It is difficult for gappers to know what approach to use with their parents. They are, of course, ridiculously anxious. This is in spite of the fact that their children know themselves to be immortal. Crime? Drugs? Booze? Dangerous sports? You can get all those in Pinner. Why should it make any difference if it is happening on the other side of the earth? The kids know they are – for the moment – safe. So there is nothing to worry about. Right?

On the other hand, the parents are an invaluable source of money and so must be kept sweet, at least to some extent. A stroppy 'rent who can't be bothered to get down to the post office and wire urgently needed funds can be the source of much fury.

And it has to be said that some gappers clearly enjoy terrifying their parents. This young woman emailed her parents from Quito, Ecuador, after a bout of illness.

✉ Hi Mum. Sorry I haven't been in contact but this is my first time out of the house for days. I've been really, really sick. I don't know what happened. It must have been something I ate, because on Tuesday night I woke up at 3.30 in the morning and started throwing up, and didn't stop till 12 hours later (that's being sick 20 times!!!). I felt so ill after, and I could only stay in bed. I was so weak I lost all fluid in my body. Today I managed to get to the doctor, and she told me I probably have gastritis, and gave me some pills, but it was expensive. She took a lot of blood tests and my stomach was all inflamed and I couldn't eat. I get the results on Monday, and so I hope everything is okay, because she told me I might have a nasty infection. But I can't lose any more weight otherwise they are going to try to put me in hospital on one of those funny drip things. I know this sounds a bit bad, but please don't worry, Mum.

Don't worry? Is she mad? Forwarding that email, her mother writes: 'This was from our eighteen-year-old daughter. She was working in Quito and the only way we could get hold of her was by email. We had no address or phone number for her. After this email, there was no news for nearly three weeks, by which time I was frantic with worry.'

A mum in West London received an email from her son, who was in Sydney. It consisted in its entirety of this:

✉ Guess what happened to me last night? We went out and were walking back to the hostel and some guy jumped out of his car and whacked me across the head with a hammer – the bit you take nails out with. Then he punched George in the face and drove off for no reason.

As his mother says, 'I guess the fact that he could email me meant he had to be okay, but it would have been nice to have been told that.' In the event, he was.

Others just rattle merrily on, oblivious to the effect they must be having back at home. This young man is in Peru and leaves his parents with, literally, a cliff-hanger.

✉ The mine tour was very eye-opening, the average life expectancy of a miner is about 40, and we met miners of 12 who are shifting 5 tons of stone per hour in awful conditions. I found it hard to breathe in there! Fact for the day – you could build a road from Potosi to Madrid with the silver that has been mined, and alongside it build a bridge with the bones of the people who have died mining it! That's nice and cheerful for you! In La Paz now, done loads of shopping because everything is so cheap, tomorrow I'm cycling the most dangerous road in the world, we start at 4,750 metres and finish at 1,500 metres over 60k, with 1,000m drops over the side of the road most of the way. Anyway, hope that has kinda filled you in on where I am and what I've been doing.

Some gappers tell their parents too much. Others tell them too little. Either can be alarming. Take this young man, who is going around the world, and downloads as little information in as short a space as he can. He begins in Brazil.

✉ Day 2, it's raining. Can you believe it, I fly halfway around the world to escape from British weather and the second day it rains. But, it is still 25 degrees and we're hardcore, so we decided to take an organized trip that takes you to the biggest 'favella' (slum) in Rio. We caned it up the mountainside on the back of some locals' motorbikes, in the pouring rain, swerving between the cars, etc., till we reached the top, then proceeded to walk down through the heart of the favella! You can really see the vast difference in wealth in Rio, we walked down narrow paths with water literally flying past our feet, as they don't have any decent drains, water was gushing down the paths, through some people's houses, yet the locals still remained friendly, happy to have their photo taken, apart from the drug dealers, when we had to put the cameras away (we were perfectly safe, Mum, I promise).

Yeah, right, as a gapper would respond to that assurance. Two months later, he gets himself from Peru to New Zealand in just over 200 crisply chosen words. Careful readers will notice a certain theme, alcohol-based.

—

⊠ Machu Picchu, amazing sight, hard but good 4-day trek, Cuzco, gr8 party town, on the piss a lot, Arequipa, saw an old mummy and got drunk again, Colco Canyon, deep canyon with lots of massive condors, Pisco, home of the national drink, pisco sours, therefore got drunk again, Ballestas Island, saw penguins and seals chillin' on the rocks, Lima, bit rubbish to be honest, flew back to Chile, Santiago, the ice cream capital of the world. NEW ZEALAND, part two of the journey, arrived in Christchurch, like England, nice but a bit boring, met Dezz and Ollie, not rich cos he's a knob and managed to lose his passport, Fox Glacier, big block of ice, cool though, Queenstown, good shit, went body-boarding down a grade 3–4 river, cold but amazing, went to Milford Sounds, got a bad day, bit rainy, back to Queenstown for the bungee, this time, The Nevis, 134 metres high, amazing again, some random place overlooking Mt Cook, gr8 hotel, heated floors and spa etc. That's just about up to where I am, going swimming with dolphins tomorrow in Kaikoura, should be good, probably missed loads out, but you'll get over it …

Of course, to the anxious parents, large chunks of that brief missive might have been written in letters of fire: their son is constantly drunk, is travelling with the kind of people who lose their passport, travels down rapids without even a boat underneath him, and goes bungee jumping from 450 feet. But at least he described these adventures after he had survived them. This is not always the case.

⊠ Birthday plans! I was planning on doing the sunset cruise

and gorge swing, but I think we are doing a bungee jump
from the highest bridge in the world (!!!). I am going to
dress very silly in a big dress so people don't forget me!
Love you all …

The sender elicits this reply from her anguished father.

✉ For God's sake, Tess, that is NOT the sort of thing you tell
your parents BEFORE you do it. Fine if you have to do it,
then go ahead, but tell us afterwards, not before.

She sends a not particularly contrite reply.

✉ Don't worry Dad!
Bungee complete.
Wow!
111 metres!
Amazing, but so scary, you really don't think you are going
to do it, but you just do! It was incredible!! Freya and I are
going to do again in tandem on Wed!! Love you lots, Tess.

Some offspring have at least a degree of sympathy with their
parents and try to keep them happy. This is not hard to do, but
not always easy to maintain.

✉ Hey Mum and Dad,
Don't fret, cos I am still alive, and you always said that was
the main thing. I should probably mention that I am not
pregnant. I am also not yet a heroin /coke /ecstasy
/morphine addict. Neither have I killed anyone. Yesterday I

saved a little boy when I thought he was drowning. I have definitely 'found myself' and also made a huge difference to the village where I am staying. I have lots of good intentions, like building wells and libraries. I have given up smoking. I have started writing poetry. I have found God. I miss you and love you all so so so much and can't wait to see you. Love Tasha.

She adds a P.S. in tiny letters, perhaps so that she can claim she gave them due warning, but hopes it might not be spotted.

✉ I may or may not have been shopping, courtesy of Daddy's magic MasterCard.

It's touching how often, 8,000 miles away, our youthful travellers can remember important events in the calendar, such as this young woman writing from northern India.

✉ Yeah, sorry for lack of contact recently, but I can explain! I was planning on ringing on Mother's Day, but our train was an unbelievable 8 HOURS late, which meant we were stuck on it for 24 hours instead of 16. And so couldn't get to a phone. Today is the first chance I've had to email. Sorry! So, yeah, Happy Mother's Day, hope you had a nice day (nicer than mine, anyway, woken up by transvestites. And then men with guns – I'm not sure which is worse!). Did you get brekkie in bed?

That news would make any Mother's Day perfect, even a delayed one. Would it not? Mind you, on occasion parents can also email anxieties from home.

—

✉ Poor Angela Houghton has broken her foot, kicked by a horse – crutches for 3 weeks – and Betty Purdue has broken her hip, so no driving, also crutches and Zimmer frame for 8 weeks, so a few crocks around. Charlie Edmonds got beaten up by some townies in Edinburgh, but is fine, though has a fractured skull so has to take things vaguely easy for a bit. Hope you enjoy Phnom Penh.

One important discovery for gappers is that – to their surprise – their parents are not invariably wrong. This young woman thought she could make big money in the US, specifically waitressing in Boston. She was mistaken.

✉ Dear Mum, I hate it when you're right. I don't know why I was surprised; I guess it was because it was a busy, fairly upscale restaurant with a sushi bar and Korean barbecue and everything, the work is pleasant, the tips are good, my supervisor's really nice and my co-workers are great. Unfortunately all of the latter are working there illegally. No $3 an hour for them, they were all promised this, but it turns out that the owner never pays anything and they live off tips alone. I will go to the owner tomorrow and demand to be paid what I was promised on a regular basis, I have the authorities on my side! This may mean that I will end up with no job. Oh well, it will mean I've lost a week in finding a job, but at least I can scam that I know how to waitress now.

Her mother adds: 'I'm terrified now that she'll fall foul of the Korean mafia.'

Often it's the little things that matter. This is from Latin America.

✉ I have NO clean clothes. Literally EVERYTHING is smelly and wet. I haven't smelled nice for a month, cos even after a shower I have to dry with a dish towel. Please, Mum, could you fly out here and do my washing?

Some gappers actually claim to heed their parents' advice, which does seem a little improbable. This is from a pair of young women travelling in Thailand, and, as you can see, it helped to inspire the title for this book.

✉ I have some time to kill before we rent a boat with some guys in our hostel and go around the island snorkelling and maybe 'cliff-jumping', only 8 metres, but you can pay 500 baht (about £10) to jump 20 metres, don't worry I'm not going to do that. Don't worry, we're renting a boat driver, as well!!! I almost got a tattoo on my foot last night but I listened to what my mother said and slept on it, and woke with a strong desire NOT to! Thank God I have such a wisdom-filled mummy!

   Yesterday I was singing Christmas carols which is so weird, cos it's so hot here! I've been riding mopeds on the beach and I fell off one. It was going slowly at the time, tho', but I have a bruise!!! DON'T TELL MUM!!! Hi, Mum, if you are reading this, the above is not true! (Dad, it completely is!)

It is extraordinary how often our travellers will drop in a single line, even a phrase, without realising what gnawing terror it is likely to cause back home. This is also from Thailand.

> ✉ Very tired, very intense, very bizarre, and slightly drunk, so will reply properly after withdrawing cash, all you have to know is I'm safe, happy, in one of the most dangerous tourist streets in the world. Well, it wouldn't be so popular if it was that dangerous. Love you, miss you, and thanks for the money …

One thing that baffles some travellers is that their parents do not necessarily share their delight in the new friends they have made. For example, imagine how you would feel if your daughter in Kenya sent you this message.

> ✉ Hey, ma, must be quick cos late. Just to warn you, met some awesome Aussies last night, who are going to London next week. I said they could stay with you, to save money. Gave them your number, hope you don't mind, they're all lovely. Can't remember names, but all (4 in total) so funny and lovely and super-fit. Xxx love you.

This email from Australia was not sent home, but it does demonstrate a sensitive awareness of paternal anxieties.

> ✉ Met a huge group of boys from Brisbane and hung out with them. Scored a fully fledged, hot surfer dude complete with pony tail and eyebrow bar, who incidentally got deported from England, can't wait to introduce him to Dad. All was going well till the last night when he never came

out to say goodbye, so I compromised and got with his friend instead, oops, didn't go down well at all.

Gappers are not always as grateful as they might be to those who gave them the precious gift of life. This is from West Africa.

✉ Let's play games. First to reply with how these words are associated with one another will get a prize:

1. Snoopy bra, Snoopy pants, size 14 see-through knickers, lilac (yes, that's a dodgy shade of purple) top, pink hairband and some cool pyjamas.

2. Not get pregnant. Earn a million pounds. Go to university and try to make some friends, get over Westlife, fit into size 8, make smoking harmless and cheaper.

3. Roast beef, washing machine, make-up/nice hair, not being sweaty, TV, crisps, butter, those Haribo strawberries, lack of rice.

Actually, sod guessing. The answers are:

1. My birthday presents from Mum and Dad. I can't believe Mum thinks I'm size 14, or that I need sexy underwear in Ghana.

2. Missions for my 19th year.

3. What I miss about home.

This is by a young man writing to his parents from China.

✉ Here's something to make my dear parents proud. On Friday we all got drunk and went bowling, for some reason me and Ed decided that it would be cool to steal one of the pins, now I don't know if you've ever tried to do this, but let me tell you – it's tricky. We thought about it for a while, trying to come up with a cunning way of doing it without being seen or getting killed by the pin picking-up machine, but as we were both pretty levered by this time, it ended with Ed sliding himself into the pins and blocking the machine, and me crawling in to grab one. So now I'm the owner of a genuine bowling pin, signed by Ed, the mentally insane Australian. And don't bother complaining to me about this behaviour, blah blah blah, because I'm probably going to do it again next weekend when 3 gap lads come to visit. Yes, I know I'm very immature, etc., but who cares? They have different laws for foreigners out here, do you know that someone could be given the death penalty if they stole from me? So don't worry.

And what parents wouldn't find the cockles of their hearts gently aglow at that news? 'My son is engaged in demented, dangerous larceny – but at least anyone who nicked his wallet would be shot through the head and his family charged for the bullet.' The same young man gets himself a Chinese girlfriend and is invited to meet her parents for dinner.

✉ I told them about you and mum, I tried to say you were fifty and that you were a teacher, but unfortunately the Chinese word for 'teacher' and the word for 'rat' are almost identical, so I said, 'my dad is a 50-year-old rat'. Her dad nearly died laughing. Liu spent the evening telling them stupid things about me, e.g. when I asked her dad if I could have the beer bottle top for me and Del's collection, she told him I wanted to chew on it while I watch TV. She's a funny girl ...

Now and then we get a glimpse of parents' reactions to all this news. This is to a gapper in South America from her mum.

✉ It was lovely to hear from you so soon. I am trying to imagine what it must be like to sleep with the rainforest sounds around you, tucked under your mozzie net and hearing all the unfamiliar rustles and scampers, and waking in the early pre-dawn to the cacophony of forest life. You must be so busy looking after the animals at the Lodge, caring for, feeding, protecting and preparing them. Fascinating.

　　Remember, an ocelot is not a pet, and you can't have one at home.

Here is a classic example of the kind of email which a gapper should never send to their parents, even by accident. Especially by accident. The young woman was writing from Goa.

✉ Our biggest news is our new careers. We were scouted to podium dance at a new five-star hotel here. Me and Jen were seriously apprehensive, but Aly and Luce were well up for it. We would be paid 1,000 rupees [£12] to dance on a platform for two hours. It all got a bit out of hand, though. We were picked up by these headhunters, in their snazzy Land Rover, all the time thinking, God, our parents would kill us if we did this. The people said we just had to pretend to the big boss that we were professionals. After waiting an hour we went into his amazing office, all fuzzy and burned from the beach. He looked us up and down, and was not impressed. By this time we really didn't want to do it, and things started to look a bit serious. He got some costumes out, really gross Hawaiian sarongs and big baggy T-shirts, and asked us where we had danced, so I said the Grosvenor Hotel back home, and he looked quite impressed. Aly by this time did a little wee from laughing so much. We were taken to the next man, whern I said the only way we would do that was if we were drunk, he bollocked me for being so unprofessional. We asked to be taken back to our hotel, and on the way we were called and told that we looked too young. Oh, shit! We saw our 'pimp' last night who said the real reason was that our boobs were too small. For once in our lives we were grateful for our small chests. Love you all, love to everyone, xxxxx

This is a classic example of how not to leave your parents calm, collected and confident. The writer omitted to remove her mother's address before hitting the SEND button. Her adventures elicited this response.

✉ Darling, how COULD you be so stupid? Perhaps you didn't mean to send that one to your parents, but I'm glad you did. Has it occurred to you what can happen to girls who do things like that? The world (as I thought you might have realised by now) is not full of nice people, and girls who have anything at all to do with men running dodgy bars are likely to wind up dead in the bottom of a ravine. Do you remember the girl from England who disappeared in Tokyo two years ago? She thought she might like to work as a hostess in a bar. Eventually her BONES turned up in a cave outside the city. Honestly, I thought you had more common sense. It actually worried me out of my skull and it makes me want to cry just thinking about it.

Money is, of course, a constant problem and some gap-year students attempt to solve it through entrepreneurship.

✉ Dad:- You will never guess our most recent investment. We travelled here in style as we have bought a golden Mercedes. Only £150 each and we will definitely be able to sell it for more. It's also acting as our house for the moment. Glad it's raining in England. Will call soon, love Adam.

✉ Hey, Dad:- Sorry it has been a while, but guess what? We found more beaches. Here we are in Aus. No one seems to want our Mercedes. Apparently there isn't a very big market here for golden cars. Let me know if anyone wants one. Love, Adam.

✉ Hello Dad:- Do you know of anyone who wants a new car? Love, Adam.

✉ Hi Dad:- Just sold our golden car. Turned out not to be as successful an investment as anticipated. Managed to get arrested last night for 'misbehaviour', but more precisely, 'urinating next to a lamppost'. Some arsey policeman thought I was pissed. Please can you record the England football matches? More soon, love Adam.

Others do not trouble themselves even trying to raise money.

This young man in Thailand tries long-distance, electronic pan-handling.

✉ PS, it would be great if Grandpops relieved the financial burden that buying a new camera has caused to my accounts, otherwise it's debt city for me.

This young man is in China, and right out of money. He decides first to blame his bank at home.

✉ What's going on with the money? I went to the bank this evening, and the machine wouldn't give me anything, meaning that me and Alice have 19 yuan to live on, which is fuck all. We also have train tickets to Kunming leaving in two days, and if I don't have the money by then they will be wasted, because we can't leave without paying the hotel bill. Phone HSBC and tell them to sort it out NOW! Please do all this as soon as possible, I'm getting panicky about what the hell I'm going to do without any money.

Next day nothing appears to have happened, so he turns his rage upon his parents.

✉ I have 15 yuan = about £1.20, today is Sunday and whatever steps we take will take until Tuesday to finish. Thanks for doing absolutely nothing about my problems, am I right in saying that? I emailed you four or five days ago saying I was in trouble, and in the meantime you have done what? Put zero money into my account and sent me a few jokey emails. Well, from this end it's not funny, we

barely have money to eat, if the hotel finds out about this
there'll be real trouble. No, now it's time for you to actually
do something. I am not looking forward to living off packet
noodles for three days.

Dad is able to get in touch with the bank and arranges matters
so that he has £429 available. His son seems less than delighted.

⊠ After three days will I be able to use the rest of the
money, right? I trust you that this will work, I'm so tired
and depressed, I've slept about four hours in the last two
days, I've had some sort of food poisoning, eating
nothing, and every time I tried to drink water, I would
throw up straight away, I'm feeling a bit better today and
managed to eat some noodles. I really hope this is the
end of my problems.

It isn't. Five days later:

⊠ More fucking problems! I still can't access the money in my
bank. I went to buy a plane ticket today and they refused
my card, I went into their office and phoned the HSBC
credit card hotline, the robot voice told me that my balance
was £800 and today I was able to spend £100. WHAT THE
FUCK IS GOING ON? I am fed up with looking like a tosser
because my bloody card never works. ARE YOU SURE YOU
ARE PUTTING THE MONEY IN THE RIGHT PLACE?

His father makes a brave stab at sorting out his finances. It turns
out that, to cut a very long story short, the bank automatically

skims off his substantial credit card debt every month, leaving his account severely depleted. Dad concludes:

☒ The upshot of all this hoo-hah is that your accounts are a dog's dinner, a mess of declined transactions.

It turns out that, when he went to book his flight out to Tokyo, his card was refused, but the amount was nevertheless debited.

☒ Are you saying that the money has been taken but they didn't realize and so I've been ripped off?

Maybe so, maybe not. His father tries again. You can almost hear the deep breath.

☒ My magic formula says that:
  A) available credit
  EQUALS
  X) credit limit (now £1,500)
  MINUS
  Y1) old spending (£1,070 when you maxed out your card in Dali)
  PLUS
  Z) money put in to pay off credit card bill (last week I moved £660 from your current account … not the full £800 I'd put in because your current account was £140 overdrawn!!) so A=£1,090 (£1,500 minus £1,070 plus £660) as I guess in my email on Saturday …

That's the simple part of the email. You do not need to know the even more complicated sums that follow. His father finishes:

✉ Well, that's my dim and distant idea about what the hell might actually have been going on. Sorry if it's not very helpful.

Dad comes to suspect that a sneaky merchant has added an '0' to a credit card chit.

✉ Do you always know what you are signing for? I dunno, it's getting far too stressful for me too.

This answer is not thought adequate. His son replies next day.

✉ You keep complaining about my spending but the longer you fail to get this problem sorted out, the more money will get spent. Beijing is an expensive place to piss about going to banks all day, plus it is 39 degrees outside, which makes me annoyed the minute I step out of the hotel. Seriously I don't know how much longer I can last …
　　I'm fucking fed up with this, stop sending me sarcastic emails and telling me 'it doesn't add up'. I DON'T GIVE A FUCK.
　　Just go down to HSBC and don't leave until you're convinced that something has taken place which will enable me to come home … I don't care if you have to use all your savings to pay off my overdraft, or if you have to sell your car, PLEASE JUST GET ME HOME!!!!!!!!!!!!!!!!!!!!!!!!!!

Finally his father manages to persuade the bank that the problem is serious and the young man comes home.

Emily's Golden Rules

Ten top tips for the perfect gap-year email:

1. It is crucial to think of the audience. For example, when you are writing to friends it is acceptable to include details of drunken activities and misdemeanours with humorous consequences (esp. if end up in jail / randommer's house who won't let you leave / bed with someone you can't remember the name of / new country you have never heard of). Yet it is important to censor recipient list. When writing to parents / grandparents / godparents (basically anyone who would disapprove of you getting up after lunchtime or watching TV all day) be sure to keep away from describing aforementioned antics and subtly comment on how much you are doing for the orphans / invalids / children you are supposed to be helping, mixed in with obligatory appreciation of beautiful scenery and wonderful people, and you will be sure to be pleasantly surprised next Christmas as well as avoiding multiple (very tiresome) worried emails from Mum. (And vice versa of course. Your friends really don't care what you are doing to 'save the world' or about the stunning lake you just swam in – unless of course there are crocodiles and piranhas that stole your bikini etc.)

2. However, remember that when describing that abovementioned 'drunken night' or intrepid 'white-water

rafting' there are a few forbidden phrases:

Awesome – so overused and 'wannabe surfer / rasta / stoner'.

SOOO AMAZING – used far too frequently and the more ooooos on 'so' makes for less sincerity.

Literally The Coolest thing EVER – unlikely to be true.

Don't compete for longest bus ride – to be honest, all bus rides are hell, and everyone who travels has to just cope, five hours or fifteen.

Don't tell everyone quite how much you drank, or give blow-by-blow accounts of your night and the fact that a beer is only 25p – a) it's all cheap relative to England, b) It's not cool to claim you 'got so fucked, I was like puking and like drank 17 pints and then went to this really "safe" bar and then got really mashed' – it will be obvious from your stories.

Avoid exclamation marks if possible – they automatically make contents less funny. (!!!! – see).

3. Personal 'hellos' at the end of group emails can be a wonderful weapon in letting everyone know that 'Sophs – did you really shag eleven people in NZ?' and 'Ed – cannot believe you hired a prostitute'. It can also be incredibly laborious to sieve through all the 'I miss you's and 'Mum – how are the dogs?' only to find that there is no personal little message for you. Private 'shout-outs' to various friends and family are always rather annoying (or if involving interesting gossip then they are inappropriate and the likes of Sophs and Ed will be furious), and it is so much nicer getting a personal email anyway ...

4. Although cynicism is always funny, be careful. One doesn't

want to arrive back home to be branded shallow, cold-hearted and selfish. It should be remembered that the tone of your message is often hard to portray and thus decipher by the reader, and so by saying that 'x is a shit-hole full of poor people' without offering any redeeming features, it is likely you will be criticized. That charming and compassionate image that you have spent so many arduous years deceptively presenting to various extended family members at Boxing Day lunch may have all been wasted in one short note from far-away.

5. Short is sweet. Bear in mind that all of your friends will probably be paying by the hour (for their internet) and thus only allow a couple of minutes to read each email before replying. Consequently, only the occasional really exciting or amusing story can break the rule of 300 words (and even then, attention should be paid to the operative words, 'occasional, exciting, amusing'). Your friends will be much more appreciative receiving your correspondence if you 'play hard to get' and don't bombard them with long-winded descriptions and irrelevant news of what you ate for supper and what you dreamed last night. (I kid you not, this has been known to happen.) Also on this theme, don't feel the need to describe day-by-day accounts to your friends. It's common for people to start off with 'I think I last emailed from Goa, Monday was pretty much the same, Tuesday involved a walk around our town etc. etc.' Seriously boring.

6. Be prepared for your mother to forward your correspondence on to all her friends and all your relatives (simply because you have either managed to convince her that you are doing amazing

things to save the impoverished children you are living with and she is very proud, or that she finds you very funny, simply because you are her daughter / son, and parents are loyal like that). But anyway, there are some negative consequences: a) for the foreseeable future (well, until someone else goes away or does something exciting) – at every family lunch you will have to expand upon everything you wrote; b) it means you have no stories left to tell when you are one-on-one with Aunt Mary; c) no one else will enjoy them as much as your parents, who are missing their 'little petal', and everyone you have ever met of your parents' generation has had to read your petty activities and pretend to appreciate family jokes; d) in turn, 'Mum' will receive copies of her friends' children's emails, and your 'two months teaching English in India' will seem pitiful compared to 'Charlie Scott's year building igloos for very cold Eskimos'. So basically, be warned.

7. Be tactful if you need to email home and ask to 'borrow' some money. There are several ways to do this, but I reckon the most effective is to concentrate on your survival and health, e.g. eating fruit and veg, which is 'very expensive', and the dangers of staying in the cheapest hostels (i.e. mention blood on walls, no locks on door, and scary men hovering in corners and lurking outside – lurkers are always a massive worry for parents and thus an excellent blackmailing tool). Also, never comment on amazing shopping, amount of times you go out at night or the £30 it cost to get your tattoo / various piercings. End enthusiastic and mature email by mentioning the wonderful time you are having but how much you miss home etc. and how you can't wait to get back and explain how the Taj Mahal / Inca

Trail has affected your view on the world.

8. 'Decorated' stories are always more enjoyable, but one must take into account fellow travellers and their correspondence. Your friends may start to question the authenticity of your emails when they receive one from you exclaiming, 'I have spent all day in hospital, as three of us have abscesses on our feet from getting 3cm of glass stuck ... they just shoved the needle straight in and picked out every grain of sand ... it was quite simply the worst hour of my life', and ten minutes later, they receive one from your companion saying, 'Just spent the last twenty minutes in clinic cos Emma has a cut on her foot and needed the nurses to clean it – talk about hypochondriac, Savlon would have been fine.' Embellishment should be kept slight and subtle and will then be way more effective.

9. The subject line is often a good tool to make your email original and thus interesting. It's normally best to avoid the typical 'recent update' or 'news from Thailand' as anyone with another friend or any sense will immediately classify your recent account as 'junk' and will be unlikely to read it. Random snippets from your email or bizarre funny lines are always good ways of 'wooing' readers. I always find the most tempting subject lines involve scandalous news or completely random statements (e.g. 'whale wrestling in Warsaw', and the email is about doing the Inca Trail).

10. It may seem such a hassle to email people, especially parents. However, you never know when you might need a loan / bail money / favour and thus it is important to keep the 'rents sweet.

It is therefore useful to at least feign an interest in 'home life' and pretend to appreciate Mum's news that 'at last the daffodils have come out, just had lunch with Mrs Smith from next door and the downstairs loo has flooded'. Your parents will relish any correspondence, and it's an easy way to earn Brownie points.